Flying the Atlantic in Sixteen Hours

Capt. Sir Arthur Whitten Brown, K.B.E.

Flying the Atlantic in Sixteen Hours

The First Non-Stop Trans-Atlantic Flight, 1919 by
One of the Aviators

ILLUSTRATED

Sir Arthur Whitten Brown

LEONAUR

Flying the Atlantic in Sixteen Hours
The First Non-Stop Trans-Atlantic Flight, 1919 by One of the Aviators
by Sir Arthur Whitten Brown

ILLUSTRATED

First published under the title
Flying the Atlantic in Sixteen Hours

Leonaur is an imprint of Oakpast Ltd

Copyright in this form © 2021 Oakpast Ltd

ISBN: 978-1-78282-934-8 (hardcover)
ISBN: 978-1-78282-935-5 (softcover)

http://www.leonaur.com

Publisher's Notes

Contents

Some Preliminary Events   7

St. John's   16

The Start   26

Evening   36

Night   41

Morning   48

The Arrival   55

Aftermath of Arrival   60

The Navigation of Aircraft   66

The Future of Transatlantic Flight   77

The Air Age   95

CHAPTER 1

Some Preliminary Events

After me cometh a builder. Tell him I, too, have known.

Kipling.

It is an awful thing to be told that one has made history, or done something historic. Such an accusation implies the duty of living up to other people's expectations; and merely an ordinary person who has been lucky, like myself, cannot fulfil such expectations.

Sir John Alcock and I have been informed so often, by the printed and spoken word, that our achievement in making the first non-stop transatlantic flight is an important event in the history of aviation that almost—but not quite—I have come to believe it. And this half-belief makes me very humble, when I consider the splendid company of pioneers who, without due recognition, gave life, money or precious years, often all three, to further the future of aeronautics—Lilienthal, Pilcher, Langley, Eiffel, Lanchester, Maxim, the Wrights, Bleriot, Cody, Roe, Rolls and the many daring men who piloted the weird, experimental craft which were among the first to fly.

I believe that ever since Man, but recently conscious of his own existence, saw the birds, he has desired to emulate them. Among the myths and fables of every race are tales of human flight. The paradise of most religions is reached through the air, and through the air gods and prophets have passed from earth to their respective heavens. And all authentic angels are endowed with wings.

The present generation is lucky in that, despite this instinctive longing since the beginning of human history for the means of flight, it is the first to see dreams and theories translated into fact by the startling development of practical aviation, within the past fifteen years. The aeronautical wonders of the next fifteen years are likely to be yet more startling.

Five years ago, before the offensive and defensive needs of war provided a supreme *raison d'être*, flying was but a costly and dangerous pastime. As such it attracted the first-class adventurers of every race, many of whom lost their lives on weird, Jabberwock-like aircraft, built and tested before experimental data and more accurate methods of calculation became available.

But even these men could not realise the wonderful possibilities of the coming air age, of which they were the pioneers. Nearly all the early aeroplanes were born of private enterprise, for capitalists had no faith in the commercial future of flight. Very few firms applied themselves solely to the manufacture of aircraft or aero engines, and only two or three of the great engineering companies had the vision to maintain aeronautical departments.

Among the few important companies that, in those days, regarded aeronautics seriously was Messrs. Vickers, Ltd. They established an experimental department, and as a result of its work began to produce military types of aircraft which were in advance of their period. Later, when the whirlwind of war provided the impetus which swept pioneer aviation into headlong progress, the Vickers productions moved with the times, and helped largely to make the British aircraft industry the greatest in the world. Now that aviation has entered into the third phase of its advance—that of a peace-time commercial proposition—they are again in the forefront of production. Incidentally they provided me with the greatest chance of my life—that of taking part in the first non-stop flight across the Atlantic. Since then a Vickers aeroplane has won yet another great distinction—the prize for the first flight from England to Australia.

At this point I desire to pay a very well-deserved tribute to the man who from the beginning has backed with money his faith in the future of aviation. The development of aeronautics has been helped enormously by the generous prizes of Lord Northcliffe and the *Daily Mail* for the first flights across the English Channel, from London to Manchester, around the circuit of Britain, and finally across the Atlantic.

In each case the competitions seemed impossible of fulfilment at the time when they were inaugurated; and in each case the unimaginative began with scoffing doubts and ended with wondering praise. Naturally, the prizes were offered before they could be won, for they were intended to stimulate effort and development. This object was achieved.

But for the stimulus of these competitions, Great Britain, at the beginning of the war, might well have been in an even worse position as regards aviation than she was. And all who flew on active service during the first three years of the war realise what they owe to Lord Northcliffe's crusades for more and better machines, and for a more extensive use of aircraft.

Having helped to win one of the *Daily Mail* prizes, I am not going to quarrel with the principle of flying competitions. Certainly, the promise of reward brings to the surface ideas and potential powers which might otherwise lie fallow; but I do not believe the system of money prizes for spectacular flights to be altogether an economically sound proposition. It is not generally realised that as a rule the amount spent by each of the firms that enter a machine for such a contest as the transatlantic flight vastly exceeds the amount of the prize, although the money reward more than covers the expenses of the aviators who gain it.

Would it not be more practical to pay directly for research work? Anybody with vision can see some of the infinite possibilities which the future of aviation may hold, and which can only be found by painstaking and properly applied research. There are plenty of men able and anxious to devote themselves competently to seeking for yet-hidden solutions whereby flying will be made cheaper, safer and more reliable. What is especially wanted for the moment is the financial endowment of research into the several problems that must be solved before the air age makes the world a better place to live in, and, by eliminating long and uncomfortable journeys, brings the nations into closer bonds of friendship, understanding and commerce.

Apart from the honour of taking part in the first non-stop flight between America and Great Britain, I am especially pleased to have helped in a small way in the construction of a new link between the two continents to which I belong. My family is deeply rooted in the United States; but generations ago my ancestors were English, and I myself happened to be born in Glasgow.

This was in 1886, when my parents were visiting that city. I was an only child, and I was so well looked after that I caught neither a Scotch nor an American nor even a Lancashire accent; for later, between visits to the United States, we lived in Manchester. There, after leaving school, I served an apprenticeship in the works of the Westinghouse Electric and Manufacturing Company. I inherited in some degree a love of and an instinct for engineering from my father, one of the best mechanical engineers I have ever met. He helped to develop this instinct by encouraging me in everything I undertook, and by making me profit by the results of his experience.

In the works I was for a time a workman among workmen— a condition of life which is the best possible beginning for an embryo engineer. I found my associates of the workshop good companions, useful instructors and incorrigible jokers. My father's warnings, however, saved me from hours of waiting in the forge, at their direction, while a "straight hook" or a "putting-on tool" was made, and from hunting the shops for the "spare short-circuit."

I was congratulating myself on making good headway and, in articles accepted by various technical journals, was even telling my elders all about engineering, when the outbreak of war changed all my plans and hopes, and interfered with the career I had mapped out for myself. In fact, I was in exactly the same position as many thousands of other young men at the beginning of their careers.

Although, of American parentage and possessing American citizenship, I had not the patience to wait for the entry into the war of the United States. With an English friend I enlisted in the British University and Public Schools battalion, when it was formed in September, 1914. And, although at the time I had no more notion of it than of becoming President of the League of Nations, that was my first step towards the transatlantic flight.

Those were wonderful days for all concerned in the early training of our battalion at Epsom. In knowledge of drill our officers started level with us. Several times I saw a private step from the ranks, produce from his pocket the *Infantry Training Manual*, and show a lieutenant where he had gone wrong. Doubtful discipline, perhaps—but excellent practice, for most of the original privates of the U.P.S. soon became officers of the New Army.

I was gazetted a second lieutenant of the Manchester Regiment in January, 1915, and with it saw service in the trenches before Ypres and on the Somme. Then came the second step towards the transatlantic flight. I had always longed to be in the air, and I obtained a transfer to the Royal Flying Corps as an observer.

I had the good fortune to be posted to No. 2 Squadron, under Major (later General) Becke. While in this unit I first experienced the mixed sensations of being shot down. One day my pilot and I were carrying out artillery observation over Vendin la Vielle when, at a height of 8,000 feet, two anti-aircraft shells set our machine on fire. Somehow, the pilot managed to bring down his craft in the British lines; but in landing it tripped over some telephone wires and turned a somersault, still blazing at various points. We were thrown out, but escaped with a few burns and bruises.

After a short rest in England I returned to the squadron. I soon left it for good, however. One dull, snowy day a bullet perforated the petrol tank of the machine in which, with Lieut. Medlicott, I was reconnoitring behind the enemy lines. As a result, we were unable to reach the British zone. We landed in occupied territory; and I knew the deadly heart-sickness which comes to all prisoners of war during the first few days of their captivity.

I was repatriated after being a prisoner of war in Germany for fourteen months, followed by nine months in Switzerland.

Medlicott, meanwhile, made thirteen determined but unsuccessful bids for escape before being murdered by the Germans in 1918, while indulging in a fourteenth attempt.

My two years of captivity constituted, strange to say, the third step towards the transatlantic flight; for it was as a prisoner of war that I first found time to begin a careful study of the possibilities of aerial navigation. This I continued after returning to London, where, at the Ministry of Munitions, I was employed in the production of the larger aero-engines.

When, soon after the armistice, the ban on attempts to fly the Atlantic was lifted, I hoped that my studies of aerial navigation might be useful to one of the firms who were preparing for such a flight. Each one I approached, however, refused my proposals, and for the moment I gave up the idea.

It was entirely by chance that I became involved in the transatlantic competition. One day I visited the works at Weybridge of Messrs. Vickers. While I was talking with the superintendent, Captain Alcock walked into the office. We were introduced, and in the course of conversation the competition was mentioned. I then learned, for the first time, that Messrs. Vickers were considering an entry, although not courting publicity until they should have attempted it.

I sat up and began to take notice, and ventured to put forward my views on the navigation of aircraft for long flights over the sea. These were received favourably, and the outcome of the fortunate meeting was that Messrs. Vickers retained me to act as aerial navigator.

I soon learned to have every confidence in the man who was to be my pilot. He flew for years before the war, and he had a magnificent record for long-distance flying when engaged in bombing Constantinople and other parts of Turkey, with the detachments of the Royal Naval Air Service in the Eastern Mediterranean. His recent death in a flying accident took from aviation one of its most able, experienced and courageous pilots, and robbed his many friends of a splendid man.

We set to work, and, with every assistance from the Air Ministry, and the Admiralty, we soon had our apparatus and instruments ready for shipment to Newfoundland. Besides our two selves the Vickers transatlantic party consisted of ten other men from the works, and a specialist on Rolls-Royce aero-engines.

Alcock and I sailed from Southampton on the *Mauretania*, on board of which its commander—Captain Rostron—made me free of his bridge, and, as a widely experienced navigator, gave me much good advice. The Vickers-Vimy machine, with all stores, left later by a freight boat.

From Halifax, Nova Scotia, we proceeded to Port aux Basques, and thence by way of the Reid Newfoundland Railway to St. John's. There, we joined the merry and hopeful company of British aviators who, long before we arrived, had been preparing for an attempt to win Lord Northcliffe's prize.

That four of them did not forestall us was due in part to very bad luck, and in part to their whole-hearted patriotism. They wanted for their country the honour of the first transatlantic flight, whether non-stop or otherwise; and, being unable to continue the wearisome wait for good weather in face of the news that the American flying boat *N. C. 4* had reached the Azores, they made their attempt under conditions that were definitely unfavourable. Fate tripped up Raynham and Morgan at the start, when they tried to take their heavily-laden machine into the air while running over a too short space of uneven ground, with the wind crossways to it. Fate allowed Hawker and Grieve a rather longer run, but brought about their fall when they were half-way to success, owing to a mishap which, though trifling, had the same effect as a vital breakage.

It is superfluous, at this time of day, to offer public sympathy to such gallant competitors; but I seize the opportunity of expressing admiration for their splendid effort, and for the spirit that prompted it. To Hawker and Grieve we owed particular thanks in that we profited to a certain extent by what we learned from the cabled reports of their experiences. For Grieve, as an expert on aerial navigation, I have the deepest respect, and I am in full accord with his views and theories on this, my own subject.

The same sort of odds against accident that sent them into the sea might well have befallen Alcock and me. But it did not; and our freedom from it was an important factor in our good fortune. Others were the excellence of the Vickers-Vimy machine and the Rolls-Royce engine. Whatever credit is ours should be shared with them, and with Mr. R. E. Pierson, E.Sc., M.I.C.E., the designer of the Vickers-Vimy.

We have realised that our flight was but a solitary fingerpost to the air-traffic—safe, comfortable and voluminous—that in a few years will pass above the Atlantic Ocean; and even had the winning of the competition brought us no other benefits, each of us would have remained well content to be pioneers of this aerial entente which is destined to play such an important part in the political and commercial friendship between Great Britain and America.

The Late Capt. Sir John Alcock, K.B.E., D.S.C.

CHAPTER 2

St. John's

"Hawker left this afternoon."

This message was shouted by a chance-met motorist, who held up our own car as we were driving back to St. John's from Ferryland on the evening of May the eighteenth, after an unsuccessful search for an aerodrome site.

"And Raynham?" I asked.

"Machine smashed before he could get it off the ground."

We thanked the stranger for his news, and passed on to hear further details at the Cochrane Hotel, which was the headquarters of the several transatlantic flight contingents at St. John's. We had rather expected the Sopwith and Martinsyde parties to make an attempt on the eighteenth, although the conditions were definitely unfavourable. The news of the American *N. C. 4's* arrival at the Azores had spurred them to the great adventure, despite the weather. The United States flying boats were not competing for the *Daily Mail* prize; but Hawker and Grieve wanted to gain for Great Britain the honour of being the first to cross the Atlantic by air. The outcome of this ambition was the gallant effort that ended in the sea, half-way to Ireland.

While exceedingly sorry for Raynham, we were glad that Hawker had started, after his weeks of weary waiting, and we wished him all success; for with one exception there was the best possible feeling among the small colony of British aviators who had congregated at St. John's for the transatlantic competition. In any case, if Hawker succeeded and we no longer had a chance of winning the prize, we meant to demonstrate the high qualities of the Vickers-Vimy machine by flying from Newfoundland to Ireland.

We had arrived at St. John's early on the morning of May the thirteenth, being only twelve hours late on a scheduled time of twenty-seven hours for the journey from Port aux Basques. Thirteen, by the way, we regarded as our lucky number. The construction of our transatlantic machine was begun on February thirteenth, it was number thirteen of its class, and it reached Newfoundland on May twenty-sixth (twice thirteen). Our party, with the mechanics, totalled thirteen, and we arrived at St. John's on May thirteenth. Later we were disappointed at having to postpone the getaway until June fourteenth, instead of leaving on June thirteenth.

We hired a car, and, driving to Mount Pearl, began what was to be a long and difficult hunt for any kind of a field that could be improvised into an aerodrome. The uneven countryside through which we passed held out no hopes; and the company we met that evening at the Cochrane Hotel (Hawker, Grieve, Raynham, Morgan, and various officials and newspaper correspondents) were unanimous in declaring that the only suitable patches of ground had been appropriated, and that we should find no others near St. John's.

The American flying boats were at Trepassey, ready to start for the Azores, and most of the American correspondents had left St. John's to visit them. The United States airship *N. C. 5* had flown to St. John's some days before our arrival. She came in a fog, after wandering over the neighbourhood of Newfoundland for some hours, having lost herself, it was reported, owing to an error of 180° in the directional wireless bearings given her. She attracted large crowds, ourselves among them, to the bay. Later, we saw the airship steering an erratic course through the Gap, and mentally wished her commander good luck in his transatlantic ambitions. Soon afterwards we heard of her unfortunate break-away and total loss.

The departure of the N. C. flying boats sent great excitement into the small company of Britishers at the Cochrane Hotel. Hawker, Grieve, Raynham and Morgan discarded caution, and on hearing of the *N. C. 4's* arrival at the Azores risked exceedingly their chances of success by agreeing to start immediately, in a whole-hearted and plucky effort to gain for Great Britain the honour of the first flight across the Atlantic. The result was immediate disaster for Raynham and Morgan, whose small aerodrome was altogether unsuitable for a "take off" into the then wind, and magnificent failure for Hawker and Grieve, owing to a minor mishap to their engine.

Soon after the flight of the American craft, I met Commander Byrd, U. S. N., designer of the bubble sextant for aerial navigation that bears his name. We had an interesting talk on the problems and difficulties of aerial navigation, and I tried to secure from Washington a Byrd sextant. The United States Naval authorities promised to forward one from Washington; but unfortunately, owing to transport difficulties, it reached St. John's after our departure. Nevertheless, I am deeply grateful to the United States Navy Department for its courtesy and its offer of help in an enterprise that was foreign to them and non-official.

Newfoundland is a hospitable place, but its best friends cannot claim that it is ideal for aviation. The whole of the island has no ground that might be made into a first-class aerodrome. The district around St. John's is especially difficult. Some of the country is wooded, but for the most part it shows a rolling, switchback surface, across which aeroplanes cannot taxi with any degree of smoothness. The soil is soft and dotted with boulders, for only a light layer of it covers the rock stratum. Another handicap is the prevalence of thick fogs, which roll westward from the sea.

For about a week we continued the quest for a landing-ground, and we must have driven over hundreds of miles of very bad road. Growing tired of hiring cars, we bought a second-hand Buick which registered a total mileage of four hundred miles at the time of purchase. Before long we were convinced that the speedometer must have been disconnected previous to the final forty thousand miles.

The best possibilities for an aerodrome that we could find were several level strips of meadowland, about a hundred yards wide by three hundred long; whereas the Vickers-Vimy, fully loaded, might need five hundred yards of clear run into the wind. Meanwhile, although disappointment accompanied us all over Newfoundland, the pacing out of fields provided good exercise.

The evenings were mostly spent in playing cards with the other competitors at the Cochrane Hotel, or in visits to the neighbouring film theatres. St. John's itself showed us every kindness. We explored the town pretty thoroughly, and were soon able to recognise parts of it with eyes closed and nostrils open; for its chief occupation appeared to be the drying of very dead cod.

Having heard rumours that suitable ground might be found at Ferryland, we motored there on May the eighteenth, and it was while returning from yet another disappointment that we learned of Hawker's disappearance into the Atlantic mists. Excitement and anxiety about the possible fate of Hawker and Grieve spread all the world over; but nowhere was it more intense than among us at the Cochrane Hotel, who had shared their hopes and discussed their plans. We were a gloomy crowd indeed until St. John's heard the sensational story of their rescue.

Raynham, meanwhile, although very disappointed after the setback that damaged his machine, kept alight the candle of hope and the torch of determination. Before it was possible to know whether or not Hawker had succeeded, he made arrangements for repair and decided to try again. He also invited Alcock and me to use his ground for erecting the Vickers-Vimy. A similar invitation was given by Captain Fenn, now in charge of the Sopwith party.

Neither aerodrome would be suitable for our final "take off"; but we accepted Raynham's very sporting offer, and arranged to build up the Vickers-Vimy, which was expected to arrive any day, on his aerodrome at Quidi Vidi, while continuing the search for a more suitable field.

Our mechanics arrived with machine and engines on May the twenty-sixth, and we set to work at once on its erection. This was carried out in the open air, amid many obstacles and with much improvisation, sheerlegs for example, being constructed out of scaffolding poles. Raynham let us use his hangar as a store.

All the Vickers party worked hard and cheerfully from early dawn until dark, each man being on strenuous duty from twelve to fourteen hours a day. Two mechanics remained on guard each night, while the remainder drove about three miles to their billets.

During the whole of this period of a thousand and one difficulties, each mechanic gave of his best, and I cannot pay too high a tribute to those men who laboured for us so competently and painstakingly, and yet received none of the glory. Even those who were but indirectly concerned in the venture searched for opportunities of helping us. The reporters representing the *Daily Mail*, the New York *Times*, and the New York *World* were often of assistance when extra man-power was required. But for one of the American reporters—Mr. Klauber—we should have been obliged to start without an electric torch when our own failed at the last moment.

It was, indeed, a nerve-edging time until the machine approached completion. Each day produced some new difficulty. Alcock kept his head and his temper admirably, however, and his intelligent supervision of the mechanics' work was an effective insurance against loss of time.

As the parts of the Vickers-Vimy grew into the semblance of a complete aeroplane it attracted more and more visitors. Many rubbernecks, who seemed to have no other occupation, spent hours in leaning on the nearest fence and watching us. Soon we found it necessary to build a temporary enclosure round the machine. Even that did not keep the curious at a distance. We remained unworried so long as the crowd contented itself with just watching; but the visitors forced us to take special precautions against damage. The testing of the fabric's firmness with the point of an umbrella was a favourite pastime of theirs, and more than once we dispersed small parties whom we found leaning against the trailing-edges, much as Australian soldiers on leave from France used to lean against the lamp-posts of the Strand. One man held his lighted cigar against a wing, and was quite annoyed when asked to keep at a distance.

We were still unsuccessful in our search for an aerodrome. One day a telegram arrived from a landowner in Harbor Grace, offering what he called an ideal field. Alcock raced off to inspect and secure it; but when he returned in the evening his one-sided grin told me that we were still out of luck. "The ideal aerodrome" was a meadow about one hundred and fifty by three hundred yards—and the price demanded for its hire was twenty-five thousand dollars plus the cost of getting it ready and an indemnity for all damage. Land *sells* in Newfoundland at thirty-five cents an acre.

Soon afterwards a local inhabitant—Mr. Lester, who had done all our carting—offered us a field under more reasonable conditions, at a place called Monday's Pool. We found it to be a large meadow, half on a hill and with a swamp at the bottom. It possessed, nevertheless, a level surface of about three hundred yards, running east and west.

We examined and paced out four other fields on the hilltop, and found that by taking them in we could obtain a full run of five hundred yards. The owners of this additional ground wanted extortionate prices for its use, but after much haggling we closed a deal with them.

Thirty labourers, with pick and shovel, set to work to prepare the aerodrome by removing hillocks, blasting boulders and levelling walls and fences. Finally, it was completed, well within the time for the trial flight.

During the first few days spent on the erecting of the machine there was little for me to do. I unpacked and verified wireless and navigation equipment, and having rigged up a receiving station on the roof of the Cochrane Hotel, with the consent and help of Lieut. Clare, of the Mount Pearl Naval Wireless Station, I practiced the sending and receiving of wireless messages, and tuning in on various wavelengths.

Rain and high wind caused a delay of three days, during which the machine necessarily remained in the open, with tarpaulins over the engines and only a small windscreen to break the force of the gales. When better conditions arrived the body of the Vickers-Vimy grew slowly into the semblance of a complete aeroplane, spurred thereto by our impatience and the willing work of the mechanics. The wings being in place, the Rolls-Royce experts became busy, examining and checking every little detail of their motors, so that there should be no avoidable trouble on that account. Water for the radiator was filtered, and then boiled in a steel barrel.

Our day-to-day watchers from St. John's showed much interest in this boiling process, and asked many questions. They seemed content with our explanation that we were boiling the gasoline so as to remove all water. Several asked whether we filled the planes with gas to make them lighter. Others were disappointed because we did not intend to drop our undercarriage over the sea, as Hawker had done, and prophesied that such neglect would lead to failure.

The machine was ready to take the air on the morning of Monday, June the ninth, and we decided to make the first flight that same afternoon. We had meant to keep the news of the forthcoming trial as secret as possible, so as to avoid a crowd. It leaked out, however, and long before the engines were warmed up and tested a large gathering had collected at Quidi Vidi.

The weather was on its best behaviour, and our "take off" from the ground was perfect in every way. Under Alcock's skilful hands the big Vimy became almost as nippy as a single-seater scout. We headed directly westward, passing over the sea for some fifteen minutes. It was a clear day, and the sea reflected the sky's vivid blue. Near the coast it was streaked and spotted by the glistening white of icebergs and the evanescent appearances and disappearances of white-caps.

Trial observation with my navigation instruments proved them to be O. K.; but not a spark could be conjured from the wireless apparatus. The machine and motors seemed in perfect condition. Alcock turned the Vickers-Vimy, and brought us back over St. John's at a height of four thousand feet. Newfoundland from above looked even more bleak and rugged than it did from the ground; and we saw that landing grounds would be impossible on the eastern side of it.

We were to descend on the new aerodrome, which we picked out by means of a smudge-fire, lighted as a signal. Alcock made a perfect landing, in an uphill direction. The Vimy ran on, topped the brow, and was heading straight for a fence on the roadside; but the pilot saved a collision by opening up the starboard engine, which swung the craft round before she came to a standstill.

We pushed the machine down the hill to the most sheltered part of the field, pegged it down, and roped off a space round it, to keep spectators at a safe distance. The proposed hangar was unfinished, so that the Vickers-Vimy still remained in the open.

I dismounted the wireless generator for examination, and next day took it to Mount Pearl Wireless Station, where Lieut. Clare helped me to locate the fault and to remedy it.

A far more serious worry now confronted us. The fuel we had intended to carry was a mixture of gasoline and benzol, sent from England. On examination we found in it a peculiar precipitate, like a very soft resin. It was sticky, and had the consistency of India rubber wetted with gasoline; but when dry it reduced to a powder. Naturally we could not afford the risk of letting such a deposit clog our filters and perhaps, owing to stoppage of fuel supply, cause motor failure—that bugbear of every aviator who flies over long distances.

It was not definitely proved that the precipitate resulted from the mixture of gasoline and benzol; but so much depended on satisfactory fuel that we dared use none that was doubtful, and we decided to substitute pure gasoline for the mixture. The problem was how to find enough of the quality required—Shell B. Raynham, as much of a sportsman as ever, put his spare stock at our disposal; but fortunately, a newly arrived ship brought enough for our needs.

Mr. P. Maxwell Muller, who had organised our transatlantic party, also came on this boat. He is a rabid optimist, with the power of infecting others with his hopefulness; and we were glad indeed to see him, and especially to turn over to him such things as unpaid bills.

The second trial flight took place on June the twelfth. Once again everything except the wireless apparatus was satisfactory.

The transmitter worked well for a short time, but afterwards the insulation on a small transformer in the transmitter failed, giving me a violent shock. After a short time in the air, Alcock made another satisfactory landing. By now we were besieging Lieutenant Clements, the meteorological officer, for weather reports. Besides his own work he had now undertaken the duties of Major Partridge, official starter for the Royal Aero Club of London. As such he had to place the club's official seal on the Vickers-Vimy. This he did without any superfluous ceremony, his seal insuring that we should not cheat by flying from Newfoundland in one aeroplane and landing on Ireland in another.

At that period the weather reports, such as they were, indicated fairly favourable conditions for the flight, and we prepared to make the attempt immediately. At no time were the reports complete, however, owing to the delays in transmission; although Clements made the very best of the meagre data at his disposal.

We saw the Handley-Page carrying out its initial flights; but we hoped to leave on Friday, June the thirteenth, and thus show it the way across the Atlantic. We worked at high speed on several last-minute jobs. The compasses were swung, the wireless apparatus repaired, more elastic shock-absorbers were wrapped round the axles, the navigating instruments were taken on board, with food and emergency supplies.

But with all the hurry and bustle we found that everything could not be ready by Friday the thirteenth, and that a postponement until 4 a. m. on the Saturday was essential.

By Friday evening the last coat of dope was dry, and nothing had been overlooked. The only articles missing were some life-saving suits, which we were expecting from the United States. Long afterwards we discovered that these had been delivered to the Bank of Montreal, where the officials, believing that the case contained typewriters, stored it in their cellars.

Alcock and I went to bed at 7 p. m. on Friday while the mechanics remained all night with the machine, completing the filling of the tanks and moving it to the position chosen for the start. We were called before dawn, and joined them on the aerodrome at 3:30 a. m. on June the fourteenth.

FEATHERING THE WINGS—
SETTING UP THE FLIER AT ST. JOHN'S, N. F.

THE LAST TOUCHES—ADJUSTING THE BRACING WIRES

CHAPTER 3

The Start

A large black cat, its tail held high in a comical curve, sauntered by the transatlantic machine as we stood by it, early in the morning; and such a cheerful omen made me more than ever anxious to start.

Two other black cats—more intimate if less alive—waited in the Vickers-Vimy. They were Lucky Jim and Twinkletoe, our mascots, destined to be the first air passengers across the Atlantic. Lucky Jim wore an enormous head, an untidy ribbon and a hopeful expression; whereas Twinkletoe was daintily diminutive, and, from the tip of her upright tail to the tip of her stuffed nose, expressed surprise and anxiety. Other gifts that we carried as evidence of our friends' best wishes were bunches of white heather.

Strong westerly wind. Conditions otherwise fairly favourable.

Such was the brief summary of the weather conditions given us at 4 a. m. by the meteorological officer. We had definitely decided to leave on the fourteenth, if given half a chance; for at all costs we wanted to avoid a long period of hope deferred while awaiting ideal conditions.

At early dawn we were on the aerodrome, searching the sky for a sign and asking information of Lieutenant Clements, the Royal Air Force weather expert. His reports were fairly favourable; but a hefty cross-wind was blowing from the west in uneven gusts, and everybody opined that we had better wait a few

26

hours, in the expectation that it would die down.

Meanwhile, Alcock ran the engines and found them to be in perfect condition. Neither could any fault be found with the grey-winged machine, inert but fully loaded, and complete to the last split-pin.

It was of the Standard type of Vickers-Vimy bomber; although, of course, bombs and bombing gear were not carried, their weight being usefully replaced by extra storage tanks for gasoline. One of these, shaped like a boat, could be used as a life-saving raft if some accident brought about a descent into the sea. This tank was so placed that it would be the first to be emptied of gasoline. The fittings allowed of its detachment, ready for floating, while the machine lost height in a glide. We hoped for and expected the best; but it was as well to be prepared for the worst.

To make communication and cooperation more easy, the seats for both pilot and navigator were side by side in what is usually the pilot's cockpit, the observer's cockpit at the fore-end of the fuselage being hidden under a stream-lined covering and occupied by a tank.

The tanks had been filled during the night, so that the Vickers-Vimy contained its full complement of eight hundred and seventy gallons of gasoline and forty gallons of oil. We now packed our personal luggage, which consisted only of toilet kit and food—sandwiches, Caley's chocolate, Horlick's Malted Milk, and two thermos flasks filled with coffee. A small cupboard, fitted into the tail, contained emergency rations. These were for use in case of disaster, as the tail of the aeroplane would remain clear of the waves for a long while after the nose had submerged. Our mascots, also, were in this cupboard.

The mailbag had been taken on board a day earlier. It contained three hundred private letters, for each of which the postal officials at St. John's had provided a special stamp. For one of these stamps, by the way, eight hundred and seventy-five dollars was offered and refused on the Manchester Exchange within two days of the letter's delivery. They are now sold at about one hundred and twenty-five dollars apiece, I believe.

We breakfasted, and throughout the morning waited for a

weakening of the wind. As, however, it remained at about the same strength and showed no signs of better behaviour, we made up our minds to leave at mid-day.

We had planned to get away in an easterly direction, for although we should thus be moving with the wind instead of into it, the machine would face down-hill, and owing to the shape of the aerodrome we should have a better run than if we taxied towards the west. The Vickers-Vimy was therefore placed in position to suit these arrangements.

But soon we found that the gale was too strong for such a plan, and that we should have to "take off" into it. The mechanics dragged the machine to the far end of the aerodrome, so as to prepare for a westerly run.

This change was responsible for a minor setback. A sudden gust carried a drag-rope round the undercarriage, tightened one of the wheels against a petrol supply pipe, and crushed it. The consequent replacement wasted about an hour.

Still with hopes that the gale would drop during the early afternoon, we sat under the wing-tips at two o'clock and lunched, while conscious of an earnest hope that the next square meal would be eaten in Ireland.

The wind remaining obstinately strong during the early afternoon, we agreed to take things as they were and to lose no more precious time. At about four o'clock we wriggled into our flying-kit, and climbed into the machine. We wore electrically heated clothing, Burberry overalls, and the usual fur gloves and fur-lined helmets.

While Alcock attended to his engines I made certain that my navigation instruments were in place. The sextant was clipped to the dashboard facing the pilot, the course and distance calculator was clasped to the side of the fuselage, the drift-indicator fitted under my seat, and the Baker navigation machine, with my charts inside it, lay on the floor of the cockpit. I also carried an electric torch, and kept within easy reach a Very pistol, with red and white flares, so that if the worst should happen, we could attract the attention of passing ships. The battery for heating our electric suits was between the two seats.

The meteorological officer gave me a chart showing the approximate strength and direction of the Atlantic air currents. It indicated that the high westerly wind would drop before we were a hundred miles out to sea, and that the wind velocities for the rest of the journey would not exceed twenty knots, with clear weather over the greater part of the ocean. This was responsible for satisfactory hopes at the time of departure; but later, when we were over mid-Atlantic, the hopes dissolved in disappointment when the promised "clear weather" never happened.

The departure was quiet and undramatic. Apart from the mechanics and a few reporters, few people were present, for the strong wind had persuaded our day-to-day sightseers from St. John's that we must postpone a start. When all was ready, I shook hands with Lieutenant Clements, Mr. Maxwell Muller and other friends, accepted their best wishes for success, and composed myself in the rather crowded cockpit.

The customary signal-word "Contact!" exchanged between pilot and mechanics, seemed, perhaps, to have a special momentary significance; but my impatience to take the plunge and be rid of anxiety about the start shut out all other impressions that might have been different from those experienced at the beginning of each of the thousand and one flights I had made before the transatlantic venture.

First one and then the other motors came to life, swelled into a roar when Alcock ran them up and softened into a subdued murmur when he throttled back and warmed them up. Finally, everything being satisfactory, he disconnected the starting magneto and engine switches, to avoid stoppage due to possible short-circuits, and signalled for the chocks to be pulled clear. With throttles open and engines "all out," the Vickers-Vimy advanced into the westerly wind.

The "take off," up a slight gradient, was very difficult. Gusts up to forty-five knots were registered, and there was insufficient room to begin the run dead into the wind. What I feared in particular was that a sudden eddy might lift the planes on one side and cause the machine to heel over. Another danger was the rough surface of the aerodrome.

Owing to its heavy load, the machine did not leave the ground until it had lurched and lumbered, at an ever-increasing speed, over 300 yards. We were then almost at the end of the ground-tether allowed us.

A line of hills straight ahead was responsible for much "bumpiness" in the atmosphere, and made climbing very difficult. At times the strong wind dropped almost to zero, then rose in eddying blasts. Once or twice our wheels nearly touched the ground again.

Under these conditions we could climb but slowly, allowing for the danger of sudden upward gusts. Several times I held my breath, from fear that our undercarriage would hit a roof or a tree-top.

I am convinced that only Alcock's clever piloting saved us from such an early disaster. When, after a period that seemed far longer than it actually was, we were well above the buildings and trees, I noticed that the perspiration of acute anxiety was running down his face.

We wasted no time and fuel in circling round the aerodrome while attaining a preliminary height, but headed straight into the wind until we were at about eight hundred feet. Then we turned towards the sea and continued to rise leisurely, with engines throttled down. As we passed our aerodrome I leaned over the side of the machine and waved farewell to the small groups of mechanics and sightseers.

The Vickers-Vimy, although loaded to the extent of about eleven pounds per square foot, climbed satisfactorily, if slowly. Eight minutes passed before we had reached the thousand feet level.

As we passed over St. John's and Cabot's Hill towards Concepcion Bay the air was very bumpy, and not until we reached the coast and were away from the uneven contours of Newfoundland did it become calmer. The eddying wind, which was blowing behind us from almost due west, with a strength of thirty-five knots, made it harder than ever to keep the machine on a straight course. The twin-engine Vickers-Vimy is not especially sensitive to atmospheric instability; but under the then atmospheric conditions it lurched, swayed, and did its best to deviate, much as if it had been a little single-seater scout.

We crossed the coast at 4:28 p. m. (Greenwich time), our aneroid then registering about twelve hundred feet. Just before we left the land, I let out the wireless aerial, and tapped out on the transmitter key a message to Mount Pearl Naval Station:

All well and started.

My mind merely recorded the fact that we were leaving Newfoundland behind us. Otherwise it was too tense with concentration on the task ahead to find room for any emotions or thoughts on seeing the last of the square-patterned roof-mosaic of St. John's, and of the tangled intricacy of Newfoundland's fields, woods and hills. Behind and below was America, far ahead and below was Europe, between the two were nearly two thousand miles of ocean. But at the time I made no such stirring, if obvious, reflections; for my navigation instruments and charts, as applied to sun, horizon, sea-surface and time of day, demanded close and undivided attention.

Withal, I felt a queer but quite definite confidence in our safe arrival over the Irish coast, based, I suppose, on an assured knowledge that the machine, the motors, the navigating instruments and the pilot were all first-class.

The Vickers-Vimy shook itself free from the atmospheric disturbances over the land, and settled into an even stride through the calmer spaces above the ocean. The westerly wind behind us, added to the power developed by the motors, gave us a speed along our course (as opposed to "air-speed") of nearly one hundred and forty knots.

Visibility was fairly good during the first hour of the flight. Above, at a height of something between two and three thousand feet, a wide ceiling of clouds was made jagged at fairly frequent intervals by holes through which the blue sky could be glimpsed. Below, the sea was blue-grey, dull for the most part but bright in occasional patches, where the sunlight streamed on it through some cloud-gap. Icebergs stood out prominently from

31

the surface, in splashes of glaring white.

I was using all my faculties in setting and keeping to the prescribed course. The Baker navigating machine, with the chart, was on my knees. Not knowing what kind of weather was before us, I knelt on my seat and made haste to take observations on the sea, the horizon, and the sun, through intervals in the covering of clouds.

The navigation of aircraft, in its present stage, is distinctly more difficult than the navigation of seacraft. The speed at which they travel and the influence of the wind introduce problems which are not easily solved.

A ship's navigator knows to a small fraction of a mile the set of any ocean current, and from the known speed of his vessel he can keep "dead reckoning" with an accuracy that is nearly absolute. In fact, navigators have taken their craft across the Atlantic without once having seen the sun or stars, and yet, at the end of the journey, been within five miles of the desired destination. But in the air the currents either cannot be, or have not yet been, charted, and his allowance for the drift resulting from them must be obtained by direct observation on the surface of the ocean.

By the same means his actual speed over the ocean may be calculated. He finds the position of his craft by measuring the angle which either the sun or a selected star makes with the horizon, and noting the Greenwich mean time at which the observation is made. If the bearings of two distinct wireless stations can be taken, it is also possible to find his definite position by means of directional wireless telegraphy.

When making my plans for the transatlantic flight I considered very carefully all the possibilities, and decided to rely solely upon observations of the sun and stars and upon "dead reckoning," in preference to using directional wireless, as I was uncertain at that time whether or not the directional wireless system was sufficiently reliable.

My sextant was of the ordinary marine type, but it had a more heavily engraved scale than is usual, so as to make easier the reading of it amid the vibration of the aeroplane. My main

It Was Hard to Find an Aerodrome With Sufficient "Take Off"

Sightseers, If Left to Themselves, Would Have Wrecked the Machine

chart was on the Mercator projection, and I had a special transparent chart which could be moved above it, and upon which were drawn the Sumner circles for all times of the day. I carried a similar special chart for use at night, giving the Sumner circles for six chosen stars. To measure the drift, I had a six-inch Drift-Bearing plate, which also permitted me to measure the ground speed, with the help of a stopwatch. In addition, I had an Appleyard Course and Distance Calculator, and Traverse tables for the calculation of "dead reckoning."

As the horizon is often obscured by clouds or mist, making impossible the measurement of its angle with the heavenly bodies, I had a special type of spirit level, on which the horizon was replaced by a bubble. This, of course, was less reliable than a true horizon since the bubble was affected by variations of speed; but it was at least a safeguard. Taking into account the general obscurity of the atmosphere during most of the flight, it was fortunate that I took such a precaution, for I seldom caught sight of a clearly defined horizon.

I could legitimately congratulate myself on having collected as many early observations as possible while the conditions were good; for soon we ran into an immense bank of fog, which shut off completely the surface of the ocean. The blue of the sea merged into a hazy purple, and then into the dullest kind of grey.

The cloud screen above us, also, grew much thicker, and there were no more gaps in it. The occasional sun-glints on wing-tips and struts no longer appeared.

Thus, I could obtain neither observations on the sun, nor calculations of drift from the seas. Assuming that my first observations were satisfactory, I therefore carried on by "dead reckoning," and hoped for the best. From time to time I varied the course slightly, so as to allow for the different variations of the compass.

Meantime, while we flew through the wide layer of air sandwiched between fog and cloud, I began to jot down remarks for the log of the journey. At 5:20 I noted that we were at fifteen hundred feet and still climbing slowly, while the haze was becoming ever thicker and heavier.

I leaned towards the wireless transmitter, and began to send a message; but the small propeller on it snapped, and broke away from the generator. Careful examination, both at the time and after we landed, showed no defect; and I am still unable to account for the fracture. Although I was too occupied with calculations to pay much attention to moods or passing thoughts, I remember feeling that this cutting off of all means of communication with the life below and behind us gave a certain sense of finality to the adventure.

We continued eastward, with the rhythmic drone of the motors unnoted in supreme concentration on the tense hours that were to come.

CHAPTER 4

Evening

For a time Alcock and I attempted short conversations through the telephone. Its earpieces were under our fur caps, and round our necks were sensitive receivers for transmitting the throat vibrations that accompany speech. At about six o'clock Alcock discarded his earpieces because they were too painful; and for the rest of the flight we communicated in gestures and by scribbled notes.

I continued to keep the course by "dead reckoning," taking into account height, compass bearing, strength of wind, and my previous observations. The wind varied quite a lot, and several times the nose of the Vickers-Vimy swayed from the right direction, so that I had to make rapid mental allowances for deviation.

The results I made known to Alcock by passing over slips of paper torn from my notebook. The first of these was the direction:

Keep her nearer 120 than 140.

The second supplied the news that the transmitter was useless:

Wireless generator smashed. The propeller has gone.

Throughout the evening we flew between a covering of unbroken cloud and a screen of thick fog, which shut off the sea completely. My scribbled comment to the pilot at 5:45 was:

I can't get an obs. in this fog. Will estimate that same wind holds and work by dead reckoning.

36

Despite the lack of external guidance, the early evening was by no means dull. Just after six the starboard engine startled us with a loud, rhythmic chattering, rather like the noise of machine-gun fire at close quarters. With a momentary thought of the engine trouble which had caused Hawker and Grieve to descend in mid-Atlantic, we both looked anxiously for the defect.

This was not hard to find. A chunk of exhaust pipe had split away, and was quivering before the rush of air like a reed in an organ pipe. It became first red, then white-hot; and, softened by the heat, it gradually crumpled up. Finally, it was blown away, with the result that three cylinders were exhausting straight into the air, without guidance through the usual outlet.

The chattering swelled into a loud, jerky thrum, much more prominent than the normal noise of a Rolls-Royce aero-engine. This settled down to a steady and continuous roar.

Until we landed nothing could be done to the broken exhaust pipe, and we had to accept it as a minor disaster, unpleasant but irremediable. Very soon my ears had become so accustomed to the added clamour that it passed unnoticed.

I must admit, however, that although my mind contained no room for impressions dealing with incidents not of vital importance, I was far from comfortable when I first observed that a little flame, licking outward from the open exhaust, was playing on one of the cross-bracing wires and had made it red-hot. This trouble could not be lessened by throttling down the starboard engine, as in that case we should have lost valuable height.

The insistent hum of the engines, in fact, made the solitude seem more normal. The long flight would have been dreadful had we made it in silence; for, shut off as we were from sea and sky, it was a very lonely affair. At this stage the spreading fog enveloped the Vickers-Vimy so closely that our sheltered cockpit suggested an isolated but by no means cheerless room.

Moisture condensed on goggles, dial glasses and wires when, at about seven, we rose through a layer of clouds on the two-thousand-foot level. Alcock wore no goggles, by the way, and I made use of mine only when leaning over the side of the fuselage to take observations.

Emerging into the air above the clouds, I looked upward, and found another stretch of cloud-bank still higher, at five thousand feet. We thus remained cut off from the sun. Still guided only by "dead reckoning," the Vickers-Vimy continued along the airway between a white cloud-ceiling and a white cloud-carpet.

I was very anxious for an opportunity to take further observations either of the sun or of the stars, so as to check the direction by finding our correct position. At 7:40 I handed Alcock the following note:

If you get above clouds, we will get a good fix (position) tonight, and hope for clear weather tomorrow. Not at any risky expense to engines though. We have four hours yet to climb.

The altimeter was then registering three thousand feet.

All this while I had listened occasionally for wireless messages, as the receiver was still in working order. No message came for us, however, and the only sign of life was when, at 7:40, I heard somebody calling "B. M. K." Even that small sign of contact with life below cheered me mightily.

Throughout the journey we had no regular meals, but ate and drank in snatches, whenever we felt so inclined. It was curious that neither of us felt hungry at any time during the sixteen hours of the flight, although now and then I felt the need of something to drink.

The food was packed into a little cupboard behind my head, on the left-hand side of the fuselage. I reached for it at about 7:30, and, deciding that Alcock must need nourishment, I passed him two sandwiches and some chocolate, and uncorked the thermos flask. He made use of only one hand for eating and drinking, keeping the other on the control lever.

We happened upon a large gap in the upper layer of clouds at 8:30. Through it the sun shone pleasantly, projecting the shadow of the Vickers-Vimy on to the lower layer, over which it darted and twisted, contracting or expanding according to the distortions on the cloud-surface.

I was able to maintain observation on the sun for some ten minutes. The calculations thus obtained showed that if we were still on the right course the machine must be farther east than was indicated by "dead reckoning." From this I deduced that the strength of the wind must have increased rather than fallen off, as had been prophesied in the report of the meteorological expert at St. John's. This supposition was borne out by the buffetings which, from time to time, swayed the Vickers-Vimy. Up till then our average speed had been one hundred and forty-three knots.

I got my observations of the sun while kneeling on the seat and looking between the port wings. I made use of the spirit level, as the horizon was invisible and the sextant could therefore not be used.

Later, I caught sight of the sea for a few brief moments, and at 9:15 I wrote the following note to Alcock:

Through a rather bad patch I have just made our ground speed 140 knots, and from the sun's altitude we must be much further east and south than I calculated.

I continued to keep a log of our movements and observations, and at 9:20 p. m. made the following entry:

Height 4,000 feet. Dense clouds below and above. Got one sun observation, which shows that dead reckoning is badly out. Shall wait for stars and climb. At 8:31 position about 49 deg. 31 minutes north, 38 deg. 35 minutes west.

The clouds above remained constant, at a height of about five thousand feet. I was eager to pass through them before the stars appeared; and at nine-thirty, when the light was fading, I scribbled the inquiry:

Can you get above these clouds at, say, 60°? We must get stars as soon as poss.

Alcock nodded, and proceeded to climb as steeply as he dared. Twilight was now setting in, gradually but noticeably. Between the layers of cloud, the daylight, although never very good, had until then been strong enough to let me read the instruments and chart. At ten o'clock this was impossible without artificial light.

For my chart I now used an electric lamp. I switched on a tiny bulb which was placed so as to make the face of the compass clear in the dark, all the other fixed instruments being luminous in themselves. For my intermittent inspection of the engines I had to flash the electric torch over either side of the cockpit.

The clouds, both above and below, grew denser and darker. One could see them only as indefinite masses of nebulousness, and it became more and more difficult to judge how near to or how far from them we were. An entry in my log, made at 10:20, says,

> *No observations, and dead reckoning apparently out. Could not get above clouds for sunset. Will wait check by stars.*

An hour later we had climbed to five thousand two hundred feet. But still we found clouds above us; and we continued to rise, so as to be above them in time for some early observations on the stars.

It was now quite dark; and as we droned our isolated way eastward and upward, nothing could be seen outside the cockpit, except the inner struts, the engines, the red-glowing vapor ejected through the exhaust pipes, and portions of the wings, which glistened in the dim moon glimmer.

I waited impatiently for the first sight of the moon, the Pole Star, and other night-time friends of every navigator.

CHAPTER 5

Night

Midnight came and went amid sullen darkness, modified only by dim moonlight and the red radiance that spurted from the motors' exhaust pipes.

By then we must have climbed to about six thousand feet, although my log shows no record of our height at this stage. Meanwhile, we were still between upper and lower ranges of cloud banks.

At a quarter past twelve Alcock took the Vickers-Vimy through the upper range, only to find a third layer of clouds, several thousand feet higher. This, however, was patchy and without continuity, so that I was able to glimpse the stars from time to time.

At 12:25 I identified through a gap to north-eastward Vega, which shone very brightly high in the heavens, and the Pole Star. With their help, and that of a cloud horizon that was clearly defined in the moonlight, not far below our level, I used the sextant to fix our position.

This I found was latitude 50° 7' N. and longitude 31° W., showing that we had flown 850 nautical miles, at an average speed of 106 knots. We were slightly to the south of the correct course, which fact I made known to Alcock in a note, with pencilled corrections for remedying the deviation.

Most of my "dead reckoning" calculations were short of our actual position because, influenced by meteorological predictions based on the weather reports at St. John's, I had allowed for a falling off in the strength of the wind, and this had not

THE TRANSATLANTIC MACHINE—
A VICKERS-VIMY WITH ROLLS-ROYCE ENGINES

occurred. Having found the stars and checked our position and direction, the urgent necessity to continue climbing no longer existed. Alcock had been nursing his engines very carefully, and to reduce the strain on them he let the machine lose height slowly. At 1:20 a. m. we were down to four thousand feet, and an hour later we had dropped yet four hundred feet lower.

The clouds overhead were still patchy, clusters of stars lightening the intervals between them. But the Vickers-Vimy, at its then height, was moving through a sea of fog, which prevented effective observation. This I made known to the pilot in a message:

Can get no good readings. Observation too indefinite

The moon was in evidence for about an hour and a half, radiating a misty glow over the semi-darkness and tinging the cloud-tips with variations of silver, gold and soft red. Whenever directly visible it threw the moving shadows of the Vickers-Vimy on to the clouds below.

Mostly I could see the moon by looking over the machine's starboard planes. I tried to sight on it for latitude, but the horizon was still too indefinite.

An aura of unreality seemed to surround us as we flew onward towards the dawn and Ireland. The fantastic surroundings impinged on my alert consciousness as something extravagantly abnormal—the distorted ball of a moon, the weird half-light, the monstrous cloud-shapes, the fog below and around us, the misty indefiniteness of space, the changeless drone, drone, drone of the motors.

To take my mind from the strangeness of it all, I turned to the small food-cupboard at the back of the cockpit. Twice during the night we drank and ate in snatches, Alcock keeping a hand on the joystick while using his other to take the sandwiches, chocolate and thermos flask, which I passed to him one at a time.

Outside the cockpit was bitter cold, but inside was well-sheltered warmth, due to the protective windscreen, the nearness of the radiator, and our thick clothing. Almost our only physical discomfort resulted from the impossibility of any but cramped movements. It was a relief even to turn from one motor to the other, when examining them by the light of my electric torch.

After several hours in the confined quarters, I wanted to kick out, to walk, to stretch myself. For Alcock, who never removed his feet from the rudder-bars, the feeling of restiveness must have been painfully uncomfortable.

It was extraordinary that during the sixteen hours of the flight neither Alcock nor I felt the least desire for sleep. During the war, pilots and observers of night-bombing craft, their job completed, often suffered intensely on the homeward journey, from the effort of will necessary to fight the drowsiness induced by relaxed tension and the monotonous, never-varying hum of the motor—and this after only four to six hours of continuous flying.

Probably, however, such tiredness was mostly reaction and mental slackening after the object of their journeys—the bombing of a target—had been achieved. Our own object would not be achieved until we saw Ireland beneath us; and it could not be achieved unless we kept our every faculty concentrated on it all the time. There was therefore no mental reaction during our long period of wakeful flying over the ocean.

We began to think about sunrise and the new day. We had been flying for over ten hours; and the next ten would bring success or failure. We had more than enough petrol to complete the long journey, for Alcock had treated the engines very gently, never running them all out, but varying the power from half to three-quarter throttle. Our course seemed satisfactory, and the idea of failure was concerned only with the chance of engine mishap, such as had befallen Hawker and Grieve, or of something entirely unforeseen.

Something entirely unforeseen did happen. At about sunrise—3:10 a. m. to be exact—when we were between thirty-five hundred and four thousand feet, we ran into a thick bank that projected above the lower layer of cloud. All around was dense, drifting vapor, which cut off from our range of vision even the machine's wing tips and the fore end of the fuselages.

This was entirely unexpected; and, separated suddenly from external guidance, we lost our instinct of balance. The machine, left to its own devices, swung, flew amok, and began to perform circus tricks.

Until we should see either the horizon or the sky or the sea, and thus restore our sense of the horizontal, we could tell only by the instruments what was happening to the Vickers-Vimy. Unless there be outside guidance, the effect on the Augean canal in one's ears of the centrifugal force developed by a turn in a cloud causes a complete loss of dimensional equilibrium, so that one is inclined to think that an aeroplane is level even when it is at a big angle with the horizontal. The horizontal, in fact, seems to be inside the machine.

A glance at the instruments on the dashboard facing us made it obvious that we were not flying level. The air speed crept up to ninety knots, while Alcock was trying to restore equilibrium. He pulled back the control lever; but apparently the air speed meter was jammed, for although the Vickers-Vimy must have nosed upwards, the reading remained at ninety.

And then we stalled—that is to say our speed dropped below the minimum necessary for heavier-than-air flight. The machine hung motionless for a second, after which it heeled over and fell into what was either a spinning nosedive, or a very steep spiral.

The compass needle continued to revolve rapidly, showing that the machine was swinging as it dropped; but, still hemmed in as we were by the thick vapor, we could not tell how, or in which direction we were spinning.

Before the pilot could reduce the throttle, the roar of the motors had almost doubled in volume, and instead of the usual 1650 to 1700 revolutions per minute, they were running at about 2200 revolutions per minute. Alcock shut off the throttles, and the vibration ceased.

Apart from the changing levels marked by the aneroid, only the fact that our bodies were pressed tightly against the seats indicated that the machine was falling. How and at what angle it was falling, we knew not. Alcock tried to centralize the controls, but failed because we had lost all sense of what was central. I searched in every direction for an external sign, and saw nothing but opaque nebulousness.

The aneroid, meantime, continued to register a height that dropped ever lower and alarmingly lower—three thousand, two thousand, one thousand, five hundred feet. I realised the possibility that we might hit the ocean at any moment, if the aneroid's exactitude had been affected by differences between the barometric conditions of our present position and those of St. John's, where the instrument was set.

A more likely danger was that our cloud might stretch down to the surface of the ocean; in which case Alcock, having obtained no sight of the horizon, would be unable to counteract the spin in time.

I made ready for the worst, loosening my safety belt and preparing to salve my notes of the flight. All precautions would probably have been unavailing, however, for had we fallen into the sea, there would have been small hope of survival. We were on a steep slant, and even had we escaped drowning when first submerged, the dice would be heavily loaded against the chance of rescue by a passing ship.

And then while these thoughts were chasing each other across my mind, we left the cloud as suddenly as we had entered it. We were now less than a hundred feet from the ocean. The sea-surface did not appear below the machine, but, owing to the wide angle at which we were tilted against the horizontal, seemed to stand up level, sideways to us.

Alcock looked at the ocean and the horizon, and almost instantaneously regained his mental equilibrium in relation to external balance. Fortunately, the Vickers-Vimy manoeuvres quickly, and it responded rapidly to Alcock's action in centralising the control lever and rudder bar. He opened up the throttles. The motors came back to life, and the danger was past. Once again disaster had been averted by the pilot's level-headedness and skill.

When at last the machine swung back to the level and flew parallel with the Atlantic, our height was fifty feet. It appeared as if we could stretch downward and almost touch the great white-caps that crested the surface. With the motors shut off we could actually *hear* the voice of the cheated ocean as its waves swelled, broke, and swelled again.

The compass needle, which had continued to swing, now stabilised itself and quivered toward the west, showing that the end of the spin left us facing America. As we did not want to return to St. John's, and earnestly wanted to reach Ireland, Alcock turned the machine in a wide semi-circle and headed eastward, while climbing away from the ocean and towards the lowest clouds.

Chapter 6

Morning

Sunrise made itself known to us merely as a gradual lightening that showed nothing but clouds, above and below. The sun itself was nowhere visible.

We seemed to be flying in and out of dense patches of cloud; for every now and then we would pass through a white mountain, emerge into a small area of clear atmosphere, and then be confronted with another enormous barrier of nebulousness.

The indefiniteness of dawn disappointed my hopes of taking observations. Already at three o'clock I had scribbled a note to the pilot:

Immediately you see sun rising, point machine straight towards it, and we'll get compass bearings.

I had already worked out a table of hours, angles and azimuths of the sun at its rising, to serve as a check upon our position; but, as things happened, I was obliged to resume navigation by means of "dead reckoning."

A remark written in my log at twenty minutes past four was that the Vickers-Vimy had climbed to six thousand five hundred feet, and was above the lower range of clouds. For the rest, the three hours that followed sunrise I remember chiefly as a period of envelopment by clouds, and ever more clouds. Soon, as we continued to climb, the machine was traveling through a mist of uniform thickness that completely shut off from our range of vision everything outside a radius of a few yards from the wing-tips.

And then came a spell of bad weather, beginning with heavy rain, and continuing with snow. The downpour seemed to meet us almost horizontally, owing to the high speed of the machine, as compared with the rate of only a few feet per second at which the rain and snow fell.

The snow gave place to hail, mingled with sleet. The sheltered position of the cockpit, and the stream-lining of the machine, kept us free from the downfall so long as we remained seated; but if we exposed a hand or a face above the windscreen's protection, it would meet scores of tingling stabs from the hailstones.

When we had reached a height of eight thousand eight hundred feet, I discovered that the glass face of the gasoline overflow gauge, which showed whether or not the supply of fuel for the motors was correct, had become obscured by clotted snow. To guard against carburettor trouble, it was essential that the pilot should be able to read the gauge at any moment. It was up to me, therefore, to clear away the snow from the glass.

The gauge was fixed on one of the centre section struts. The only way to reach it was by climbing out of the cockpit and kneeling on top of the fuselage, while holding on to a strut for balance. This I did; and the unpleasant change from the comparative warmth of the cockpit to the biting, icy cold outside was very unpleasant. The violent rush of displaced air, which tended to sweep me backward, was another discomfort.

I had no difficulty, however, in reaching upward and rubbing the snow from the face of the gauge. Until the storm ended, a repetition of this performance at fairly frequent intervals continued to be necessary. There was, however, scarcely any danger in kneeling on the fuselage as long as Alcock kept the machine level.

Every now and then we examined the motors; for on them depended whether the next four hours would bring success or failure. Meantime, we were still living for the moment; and although I was intensely glad that four-fifths of the ocean had been crossed, I could afford to spare no time for speculation on what a safe arrival would mean to us. As yet, neither of us was aware of the least sign of weariness, mental or physical.

When I had nothing more urgent on hand, I listened at the wireless receiver but I heard no message for us from beginning to end of the flight. Any kind of communication with ship or shore would have been welcome, as a reminder that we were not altogether out of touch with the world below. The complete absence of such contact made it seem that nobody cared a darn about us.

The entry that I scribbled in my log at 6:20 a. m. was that we had reached a height of nine thousand four hundred feet, and were still in drifting cloud, which was sometimes so thick that it cut off from view parts of the Vickers-Vimy. Snow was still falling, and the top sides of the plane were covered completely by a crusting of frozen sleet.

The sleet imbedded itself in the hinges of the ailerons and jammed them, so that for about an hour the machine had scarcely any lateral control. Fortunately, the Vickers-Vimy has plenty of inherent lateral stability; and, as the rudder controls were never clogged by sleet, we were able to carry on with caution.

Alcock continued to climb steadily, so as to get above the seemingly interminable clouds and let me have a clear sky for purposes of navigation. At five o'clock, when we were in the levels round about eleven thousand feet, I caught the sun for a moment—just a pin-point glimmer through a cloud-gap. There was no horizon; but I was able to obtain a reading with the help of my Abney spirit level.

This observation gave us a position close to the Irish coast. Yet I could not be sure of just where we were on the line indicated by it. We therefore remained at eleven thousand feet until, at 7:20 a. m., I had definitely fixed the position line. This accomplished, I scribbled the following message and handed it across to the pilot:

We had better go lower down, where the air is warmer, and where we might pick up a steamer.

Just as we had started to nose downward, the starboard motor began to pop ominously, as if it were backfiring through one of

A Special Kind of Gasoline Had to Be Used

All Aboard for the First Trial Flight

its carburettors. Alcock throttled back while keeping the machine on a slow glide. The popping thereupon ceased.

By eight o'clock we had descended from eleven thousand to one thousand feet, where the machine was still surrounded by cloudy vapor. Here, however, the atmosphere was much warmer, and the ailerons were again operating.

Alcock was feeling his way down gently and alertly, not knowing whether the cloud extended to the ocean, nor at what moment the machine's undercarriage might touch the waves. He had loosened his safety belt, and was ready to abandon ship if we hit the water. I myself felt uncomfortable about the danger of sudden immersion, for it was very possible that a change in barometric conditions could have made the aneroid show a false reading.

But once again we were lucky. At a height of five hundred feet the Vickers-Vimy emerged from the pall of cloud, and we saw the ocean—a restless surface of dull grey. Alcock at once opened up the throttles, and both motors responded. Evidently a short rest had been all that the starboard motor needed when it began to pop, for it now gave no further signs of trouble.

I reached for the Drift Bearing Plate, and after observation on the ocean, found that we were moving on a course seventy-five degrees true, at one hundred and ten knots ground speed with a wind of thirty knots from the direction of two hundred and fifteen degrees true. I had been reckoning on a course of seventy-seven degrees true, with calculations based on our midnight position; so that evidently, we were north of the prescribed track. Still, we were not so far north as to miss Ireland, which fact was all that mattered to any extent.

In my correction of the compass bearing, I could only guess at the time when the wind had veered from its earlier direction. I made the assumption that the northerly drift had existed ever since my sighting on the Pole Star and Vega during the night, and I reckoned that our position at eight o'clock would consequently be about fifty-four degrees N. latitude, ten degrees thirty min. W. longitude. Taking these figures, and with the help of the navigation machine, which rested on my knees, I calculated that our course to Galway was about one hundred and twenty-five degrees true. Allowing for variation and wind I therefore set a compass course of one hundred and seventy degrees, and indicated to the pilot the necessary change in direction by means of the following note and diagram:

Make course

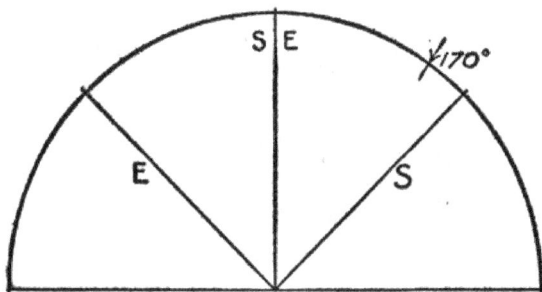

Don't be afraid of going S. We have had too much N. already.

Alcock nodded and ruddered the Vickers-Vimy around gently, until its compass showed a reading of 170 degrees.

My calculations, if correct, proved that we were quite close to Ireland and journey's end. As we flew eastward, just below the lowest clouds and from two hundred to three hundred feet above the sea, we strained our eyes for a break in the monotonous *vista* of grey waves; but we could find not even a ship.

Although neither of us felt hungry, we decided to breakfast at eight o'clock, partly to kill time and partly to take our minds from the rising excitement induced by the hope that we might sight land at any instant. I placed a sandwich, followed by some chocolate, in Alcock's left hand. His right hand remained always on the control lever and his feet on the rudder bar.

At no time during the past sixteen hours had the pilot's hands and feet left the controls. This was a difficult achievement for such a long period, especially as a rubber device, fitted to ease the strain, proved to be valueless. Elastic, linked to a turnbuckle, had been attached to the control lever and rudder bar; but in the hurry that preceded our departure from St. John's, the elastic was cut too short. All the weight of the controls, therefore, bore directly on the pilot.

The machine now tended to sag downward, being nose-heavy because its incidence had changed, owing to the gradual alteration in the centre of gravity as the rear gasoline tanks emptied. Alcock was thus obliged to exert continuous backward pressure on the control lever.

I had screwed on the lids of the thermos flask, and was placing the remains of the food in the tiny cupboard behind my seat, when Alcock grabbed my shoulder, twisted me round, beamed excitedly, and pointed ahead and below. His lips were moving, but whatever he said was inaudible above the roar of the motors.

I followed the direction indicated by his outstretched forefinger; and, barely visible through the mist, it showed me two tiny specks of—*land*. This happened at 8:15 a. m. on June 15th.

With a light heart, I put away charts and tables of calculation, and disregarded the compass needle. My work as navigator of the flight was at an end.

CHAPTER 7

The Arrival

Alcock flew straight for the specks of land, which revealed themselves as two tiny islands—Ecshal and Turbot, as we afterwards discovered. In his log of the return flight, from New York to Norfolk, of the British airship *R-34*, Brigadier-General Maitland, C. M. G., D. S. O., notes the curious coincidence that his first sight of land was when these same two islands appeared on the starboard bow of the dirigible.

From above the islands the mainland was visible, and we steered for the nearest point on it. The machine was still just underneath the clouds, and flying at two hundred and fifty feet; from which low height I saw plainly the white breakers foaming on to the shore. We crossed the coast of Ireland at 8:25 a. m.

I was then uncertain of our exact location, and suggested to Alcock that the best plan would be to find a railway line and follow it south. A few minutes later, however, the wireless masts at Clifden gave the key to our position. To attract attention, I fired two red flares from the Very pistol; but as they seemed to be unnoticed from the ground, we circled over the village of Clifden, about two miles from the wireless station.

Although slightly off our course when we reached the coast, we were in the direct line of flight for Galway, at which place I had calculated to hit Ireland. Not far ahead we could see a cluster of hills, with their tops lost in low-lying clouds.

Here and elsewhere the danger of running into high ground hidden from sight by the mist would have been great, had we continued to fly across Ireland. Alcock, therefore, decided to land.

If the atmosphere had been clearer, we could easily have reached London before touching earth, for the tanks of the Vickers-Vimy still contained enough gasoline to keep the machine in the air for ten hours longer. Thus, had we lost our way over the ocean, there would have been a useful margin of time for cruising about in search of ships.

Having made up our minds to land at once, we searched below for a smooth stretch of ground. The most likely looking place in the neighbourhood of Clifden was a field near the wireless station. With engines shut off, we glided towards it, heading into the wind.

Alcock flattened out at exactly the right moment. The machine sank gently, the wheels touched earth and began to run smoothly over the surface. Already I was indulging in the comforting reflection that the anxious flight had ended with a perfect landing. Then, so softly as not to be noticed at first, the front of the Vickers-Vimy tilted inexplicably, while the tail rose. Suddenly the craft stopped with an unpleasant squelch, tipped forward, shook itself, and remained poised on a slant, with its fore-end buried in the ground, as if trying to stand on its head.

I reached out a hand and arm just in time to save a nasty bump when the shock threw me forward. As it was, I only stopped a jarring collision with the help of my nose. Alcock had braced himself against the rudder control bar. The pressure he exerted against it to save himself from falling actually bent the straight bar, which was of hollow steel, almost into the shape of a horseshoe.

Deceived by its smooth appearance, we had landed on top of a bog; which misfortune made the first non-stop transatlantic flight finish in a crash. It was pitiful to see the distorted shape of the aeroplane that had brought us from America, as it sprawled in ungainly manner over the sucking surface. The machine's nose and its lower wings were deep in the bog. The empty cockpit in front, used in a Vickers-Vimy bomber by the observer, was badly bent; but, being of steel, it did not collapse. Quite possibly we owe our lives to this fact. In passing, and while gripping firmly my wooden penholder (for the year is not yet over), I consider it extraordinary that no lives have been lost in the transatlantic flights of 1919.

The leading edge of the lower plane was bent in some places and smashed in others, the gasoline connections had snapped, and four of the propeller blades were buried in the ground, although none were broken. That about completed the record of preliminary damage.

We had landed at 8:40 a. m., after being in the air for sixteen hours and twenty-eight minutes. The flight from coast to coast, on a straight course of one thousand six hundred and eighty nautical miles, lasted only fifteen hours and fifty-seven minutes, our average speed being one hundred and five to one hundred and six knots. For this relatively rapid performance, a strong following wind was largely responsible.

As a result of the burst connections from tank to carburettor, gasoline began to swill into the rear cockpit while we were still inside it. Very fortunately the liquid did not ignite. Alcock had taken care to switch off the current on the magnetos, as soon as he realised that a crash was imminent, so that the sparks should have no chance of starting a fire.

We scrambled out as best we could, and lost no time in salving the mailbag and our instruments. The gasoline rose rapidly, and it was impossible to withdraw my chart and the Baker navigating machine before they had been damaged.

I then fired two white Very flares, as a signal for help. Almost immediately a small party, composed of officers and men belonging to the military detachment at Clifden, approached from the wireless station.

"Anybody hurt?"—the usual inquiry when an aeroplane is crashed—was the first remark when they arrived within shouting distance.

"No."

"Where you from?"—this when they had helped us to clear the cockpit.

"America."

Somebody laughed politely, as if in answer to an attempt at facetiousness that did not amount to much, but that ought to be

taken notice of, anyhow, for the sake of courtesy. Quite evidently nobody received the statement seriously at first. Even a men-
tion of our names meant nothing to them, and they remained
unconvinced until Alcock showed them the mailbag from St.
John's. Then they relieved their surprised feelings by spontane-
ous cheers and painful hand-shakes, and led us to the officers'
mess for congratulations and hospitality.

Burdened as we were with flying kit and heavy boots, the
walk over the bog was a dragging discomfort. In addition, I suddenly discovered an intense sleepiness, and could easily have let
myself lose consciousness while standing upright.

Arrived at the station, our first act was to send telegrams to
the firm of Messrs. Vickers, Ltd., which built the Vickers-Vimy,
to the London *Daily Mail*, which promoted the transatlantic
competition, and to the Royal Aero Club, which controlled it.

My memories of that day are dim and incomplete. I felt a
keen sense of relief at being on land again; but this was coupled with a certain amount of dragging reaction from the tense
mental concentration during the flight, so that my mind sagged.
I was very sleepy, but not physically tired.

We lurched as we walked, owing to the stiffness that resulted
from our having sat in the tiny cockpit for seventeen hours.
Alcock, who during the whole period had kept his feet on the
rudder bar and one hand on the control lever, would not con-
fess to anything worse than a desire to stand up for the rest of
his life—or at least until he could sit down painlessly. My hands
were very unsteady. My mind was quite clear on matters per-
taining to the flight, but hazy on extraneous subjects. After having listened so long to the loud-voiced hum of the Rolls-Royce
motors, made louder than ever by the broken exhaust pipe on
the starboard side, we were both very deaf, and our ears would
not stop ringing.

Later in the day we motored to Galway with a representative
of the London *Daily Mail*. It was a strange but very welcome
change to see solid objects flashing past us, instead of miles upon
monotonous miles of drifting, cloudy vapor.

Several times during that drive I lost the thread of connection with tangible surroundings, and lived again in near retrospect the fantastic happenings of the day, night and morning that had just passed. Subconsciously I still missed the rhythmic, relentless drone of the Rolls-Royce aero-engines. My eyes had not yet become accustomed to the absence of clouds around and below, and my mind felt somehow lost, now that it was no longer pre-occupied with heavenly bodies, horizon, time, direction, charts, drift, tables of calculations, sextant, spirit level, compass, aneroid, altimeter, wireless receiver and the unexpected.

For a while, in fact, the immediate past seemed more promi-nent than the immediate present. Lassitude of mind, coupled with reaction from the long strain of tense and unbroken con-centration on one supreme objective, made me lose my grip of normal continuity, so that I answered questions mechanically and wanted to avoid the effort of talk. The outstanding events and impressions of the flight—for example the long spin from four thousand to fifty feet, and the sudden sight of the white-capped ocean at the end of it—passed and repassed across my consciousness. I do not know whether Alcock underwent the same mental processes, but he remained very silent. Above all I felt the need of re-establishing normal balance by means of sleep.

The wayside gatherings seemed especially unreal—almost as if they had been scenes on the film. By some extraordinary method of news transmission, the report of our arrival had spread all over the district, and in many districts between Clifden and Galway curious crowds had gathered. Near Galway we were stopped by another automobile, in which was Major Mays of the Royal Aero Club, whose duty it was to examine the seals on the Vickers-Vimy, thus making sure that we had not landed in Ireland in a machine other than that in which we left New-foundland. A reception had been prepared at Galway; but our hosts, realising how tired we must be, considerately made it a short and informal affair. Afterwards we slept—for the first time in over forty hours.

CHAPTER 8

Aftermath of Arrival

Alcock and I awoke to find ourselves in a wonderland of seeming unreality—the product of violent change from utter isolation during the long flight to unexpected contact with crowds of people interested in us.

To begin with, getting up in the morning, after a satisfactory sleep of nine hours, was strange. In our eastward flight of two thousand miles we had overtaken time, in less than the period between one sunset and another, to the extent of three and a half hours. Our physical systems having accustomed themselves to habits regulated by the clocks of Newfoundland, we were reluctant to rise at 7 a. m.; for subconsciousness suggested that it was but 3:30 a. m.

This difficulty of adjustment to the sudden change in time lasted for several days. Probably it will be experienced by all passengers traveling on the rapid trans-ocean air services of the future—those who complete a westward journey becoming early risers without effort, those who land after an eastward flight becoming unconsciously lazy in the mornings, until the jolting effect of the dislocation wears off, and habit has accustomed itself to the new conditions.

Then, after breakfast—eaten in an atmosphere of the deepest content—there began a succession of congratulatory ovations. For these we were totally unprepared; and with our relaxed minds, we could not easily adapt ourselves to the conditions attendant upon being magnets of the world's attentive curiosity.

First came a reception from the town of Galway, involving

THE VICKERS-VIMY TRANSATLANTIC MACHINE IN THE AIR

THE LAST SQUARE MEAL IN AMERICA WAS EATEN NEAR THE
WINGS OF THE MACHINE

many addresses and the presentation of a memento in the form of a Claddagh ring, which had historical connections with a landing on the coast of Ireland thereabouts by vessels of the Spanish Armada.

The warm-hearted crowd that we found waiting at Galway Station both amazed and daunted us. We were grateful for their loud appreciation, but scarcely able to respond to it adequately. Flowers were offered, and we met the vanguard of the autograph hunters. We must have signed our names hundreds of times during the journey to Dublin—on books, cards, old envelopes and scraps of paper of every shape and every state of cleanliness. This we did wonderingly, not yet understanding why so many people should ask for our signatures, when three days earlier few people had heard of our names.

The men, women and children that thronged every station on the way to Dublin seemed to place a far higher value on our success than we did ourselves. Until now, perhaps, we had been too self-centred to realise that other people might be particularly interested in a flight from America to England. We had finished the job we wanted to do, and could not comprehend why it should lead to fuss.

Now, however, I know that the crowds saw more clearly than I did, and that their cheers were not for us personally, but for what they regarded as a manifestation of the spirit of adventure, the True Romance—call it what you will. For the moment this elusive ideal was suggested to them by the first non-stop journey by air across the Atlantic, which we had been fortunate enough to make.

At one station, where a military band played our train in and out again, a wooden model of an aeroplane was presented to Alcock by a schoolboy. At Dublin, reached on the morning of Trinity Sunday, Alcock and I passed with difficulty through the welcoming crowds, and drove towards the Automobile Club in separate cars. In due course, I reached sanctuary; but where was Alcock? We waited and waited, and finally sent out scouts to search for him. They came back with the news that he had been kidnapped, and taken to Commons in Trinity College.

Landing at Holyhead next morning, we were welcomed back to the shores of England by Mr. R. K. Pierson, designer of our Vickers-Vimy machine, by Captain Vickers, of the famous firm that built it, and by Mr. C. Johnson, of the Rolls-Royce Company that supplied our motors. Scenes all along the line to London were a magnified repetition of those from Galway to Dublin. Chester, Crewe, Rugby and other towns each sent its Mayor or another representative to the station. Aeroplanes escorted the train all the way to London. Again, we could only play our part in a more or less dazed state of grateful wonder.

Of the warm-hearted welcome of the people of London, I have confused recollections that include more receptions, more and larger crowds, more stormy greetings, and an exciting, pleasant drive to the Royal Aero Club. Alcock delivered to the postal authorities the mailbag from St. John's, with regrets that it had not been possible to fly direct to London with the letters. In the evening we separated, Alcock to see a big prize fight, I to visit my *fiancée*.

Perhaps the welcome that we appreciated most was that given us next day when, at the Weybridge works of the Vickers Company, we were cheered and cheered by the men and girls who had built our transatlantic craft. We were glad indeed to be able to tell them and the designer of the machine that their handiwork had stood a difficult test magnificently, as had the Rolls-Royce engines. One of my most sincere reasons for satisfaction was that the late Mr. Albert Vickers, one of the founders of the great firm, regarded the flights as having maintained the Vickers tradition of efficiency, originality and good workmanship.

That Lieutenant-Commander Read, U.S.N., who commanded the American flying boat *N. C. 4* in its flight from America to England, had left London before our arrival was a cause of real regret. Both Alcock and I were anxious to meet him and his crew, so that we might compare our respective experiences of aerial navigation and of weather conditions over the Atlantic. The United States aviators who flew to Europe, and those that were so unlucky in coming to grief at the Azores, showed themselves to be real sportsmen; and without any exception, there was the best possible feeling between them and all the British aviators who made, or attempted to make, a non-stop journey from Newfoundland to Ireland.

Although I am supremely glad to have had the opportunity of flying the Atlantic by aeroplane, afterthoughts on the risks and chances taken have convinced me that, while our own effort may have been useful as a pioneer demonstration, single or twin-engine aircraft are altogether unsuitable for trans-ocean voyages. We were successful—yes. But a temporary failure of either of our motors (although this is unlikely when dealing with Rolls-Royce or other first-class aero motors) would have meant certain disaster and likely death.

Another vital drawback of the smaller machines is that so much space, and so much disposable lift, is needed for fuel that the number of persons on board must be limited to two, or in some cases three, and no freight can be taken. Yet another is that should the navigator of an aeroplane make an important error in calculation while flying over the ocean in fog or mist, an enforced descent into the water, after the limited quantity of fuel has been expended over a wrong course, is more than possible.

In the present condition of practical aeronautics, the only heavier-than-air craft likely to be suitable for flying the Atlantic are the large flying boats now being built by various aircraft companies; and even they are limited as to size by certain definite formulæ. The development in the near future of long flights over the ocean would seem, therefore, to be confined to lighter-than-air craft.

In this connection the two voyages across the Atlantic of the British government airship *R-34*, not long after Alcock and I had returned to London, was a big step towards the age of regular air service between Britain and America. With five motors the *R-34* could carry on if one, or even two of them were out of action. In fact, on its return flight, one motor broke down beyond the possibility of immediate repair; although there were ample facilities and an ample crew for effecting immediate repairs in the air. Yet she completed her journey without difficulty. With a disposable lift of twenty-nine tons, the airship carried plenty of fuel for all contingencies, an adequate crew, and heavy wireless apparatus that could not have been fitted on the larger aeroplanes.

Despite all this preliminary weight, a large collection of parcels, letters and newspapers were taken from America to England in record time. Had the weather conditions been at all suitable she could easily have brought the mail direct from New York to London by air. All honour to General Maitland, Major Scott and the other men who carried out this astonishing demonstration so early as July, 1919.

Even vessels of the *R-34* type, however, are quite unsuitable for regular traffic across the Atlantic. Much bigger craft will be needed if the available space and the disposable lift are to be sufficient for the carrying of freight or passengers on a commercial basis. Already the construction of airships two and a half and five times the size of the *R-34*, with approximate disposable lifts of one hundred and two hundred tons respectively, is projected. When such craft are accomplished facts, and when further progress has been made in solving weather and navigation problems, we may look for transatlantic flights on a commercial basis.

CHAPTER 9

The Navigation of Aircraft

I do not claim to be an especial authority on the theory of navigation—indeed, it was as a prisoner of war that I first took up seriously the study of that science. But I believe that sustained and sufficient concentration can give a man what he wants; and on this assumption I decided to learn whatever might be learned about navigation as applied to aircraft. As yet, like most aspects of aeronautics, this is rather indefinite, although research and specially adapted instruments will probably make it as exact as marine navigation.

Navigation is the means whereby the mariner or aviator ascertains his position on the surface of the earth, and determines the exact direction in which he must head his craft in order to reach its destination.

The methods of navigation employed by mariners are the result of centuries of research and invention, but have not yet reached finality—witness the introduction within the last few years of the Gyroscopic Compass and the Directional Wireless Telegraph Apparatus, as well as of improved methods of calculation.

In short journeys over land by aeroplane or airship the duties of a navigator are light, so long as he can see the ground and check his progress towards the objective by observation and a suitable map.

But for long distance flights, especially over the ocean and under circumstances whereby the ground cannot be seen, the navigator of the air borrows much from the navigator of the sea.

He makes modifications and additions, necessitated by the different conditions of keeping to a set course through the atmosphere and of keeping to a set course through the ocean but the principles underlying the two forms of navigation are identical.

It is impossible to explain aerial navigation without seeming to paraphrase other writers on the subject. One of the simplest explanations of the science is that of Lieutenant Commander K. Mackenzie Grieve in *Our Atlantic Attempt*, which he wrote in collaboration with Mr. Harry Hawker, his pilot, after their glorious attempt to win the London *Daily Mail's* transatlantic competition.

The chief differences between the navigation of aircraft and the navigation of seacraft are occasioned by:

(a) The vastly greater speed of aircraft, necessitating more frequent observations and quicker methods of calculation.

(b) The serious drift caused by the wind. This may take aircraft anything up to forty or more miles off the course in each hour's flying, according to the direction and strength of the wind. In cloudy weather, or at night, a change in the wind can alter the drift without the knowledge of the navigator. Hence, special precautions must be taken to observe the drift at all possible times.

(c) The absence of need for extreme accuracy of navigation in the air, since a ten or even twenty-mile error from the destination in a long journey is permissible. Another favourable point is that rocks, reefs and shoals need not be avoided. This permits the aerial navigator to use short cuts and approximations in calculation, which would be criminal in marine navigation.

There are three methods of aerial navigation—"Dead Reckoning," Astronomical Observation, and Directional Wireless Telegraphy. None should be used alone; for although accuracy may be obtained with any single method, it is highly advisable to check each by means of the others.

As in the case of marine navigation, a reliable compass, either of the magnetic or gyroscopic type, is essential for aerial navigation, as well as an accurate and reliable chronometer. Suitable charts must be provided, showing all parts of the route to be covered. When the magnetic compass is used, such charts should show the variation between True and Magnetic North at different points on the route.

NAVIGATION BY "DEAD RECKONING"

"Dead Reckoning" is the simplest method of navigation; and, under favourable conditions, it gives a high degree of accuracy. A minimum of observation is required, but careful calculation is essential.

The "Dead Reckoning" position of an aeroplane or airship at any time is calculated from its known speed and direction over the surface of the earth or ocean, and its known course as indicated by the magnetic or gyroscopic compass.

To determine the direction of movement of an aeroplane or airship, as apart from the direction in which it is headed, an instrument known as a Drift Indicator, or Drift Bearing Plate, is used.

One form of Drift Indicator consists of a simple dial, with the centre cut away and a wire stretched diametrically across it. The outer edge of the dial is divided into degrees, in a similar manner to that of the compass. It is mounted in such a way that an observer can, by looking through the centre of the disc, see the ground or ocean below him. The disc is then turned until objects on the ground—or white-caps, icebergs, ships, or other objects visible on the surface of the ocean—are seen to move parallel with the wire, without in any way deviating from it. The angle which the wire then makes with the direction in which the nose of the aeroplane or airship is pointing gives the angle of drift.

The ground speed (or speed over the surface of the earth) of aircraft can be measured by observing the time taken in passing over any fixed or very slowly moving object, while a certain angular distance is described—this being found by suitable sights, attached to the Drift Bearing Plate. From the result, considered in conjunction with the height of the aeroplane or airship, the actual speed over the surface is calculated. This speed will be in the direction shown by the wire of the Drift Bearing Plate.

The ground speed so found will differ nearly always from the air speed, as shown by the air speed meter, because of the effect of the wind. The difference is greater or less according to the wind's relation to the direction in which the aeroplane or airship is headed.

Having found by observation the drift, the ground speed and the air speed, a simple instrument such as the Appleyard Course and Distance Calculator then permits the aerial navigator to discover without difficulty, as on a slide rule, the strength and direction of the wind. Should the actual track of aircraft over the earth's surface not coincide with the desired course, the Course and Distance Calculator, or a similar instrument, can thus be used to calculate, in connection with the wind velocity and direction already found, the direction in which the nose of the craft must be pointed in order to correct the deviation due to drift.

Knowing the latitude and longitude of the point of departure, and noting carefully the time that elapses between each separate observation of the ground speed and of the course, the air navigator, with the aid of a specially prepared set of "traverse tables" (as used by mariners), can easily plot on his chart the distance covered and the direction in which it has been covered. Hence the position of the aircraft at any time is either known definitely, or can be forecast with a fair degree of accuracy.

For aerial navigation by means of "Dead Reckoning," frequent observations of ground speed and drift are necessary. If aircraft are cut off by clouds or fog from all possibility of sighting the surface of the earth, grave errors may occur, since in long distance flights the wind's velocity and direction often change without the pilot's knowledge.

Navigation by Astronomical Observation

In navigation by astronomical observation, the position of the aeroplane or airship is found by observing the height above the horizon of either the sun or another heavenly body, such as a star that is easy of recognition. The method depends upon the known fact that at any given instant the sun is vertically above

The Late Capt. Sir John Alcock Just Before Starting

Shipping the First Direct Transatlantic Air Mail

some definite point on the earth's surface. This point can be calculated from the time of the observation and the declination and equation of time, as tabulated in the nautical almanac.

In the case of stars, the right ascension of the sun and of the star also enter into the calculation. The method of carrying out such calculations is too involved for the scope of this volume, and the reader is referred to many of the excellent text books published on the subject of navigation.

Since the navigator knows, from the time of his observation, the point on the earth's surface over which is the heavenly body in question, it is clear that around this point circles on the surface of the earth may be described. From any point in any one circle the heavenly body will appear to have the same altitude or elevation above the horizon. A single observation of the altitude of any one heavenly body shows, therefore, only that the observer may be at any point on such a circle of equal altitude—otherwise known as a Sumner circle. But it does not fix that point.

A second simultaneous observation, of a different heavenly body, will give a different circle, corresponding to the position of the second body. The intersection of these two circles determines the point of observation.

This fact constitutes a reliable basis for fixing one's position during a clear night, when many stars are visible and choice of suitable heavenly bodies may be made. During the day, however, the light of the sun prevents other heavenly bodies from being seen, so that only a single observation is possible.

If the aeroplane or airship were not moving, then two successive observations of the sun, with an interval of an hour or more between them, would give the intersecting circles and fix the position. But the aircraft being in motion, it is necessary to combine the method of "Dead Reckoning" with the use of the Sumner circles, as found by observation of the sun's altitude.

In order to avoid drawing the entire circle, a small portion only of it is shown on the chart—so small that it may be regarded as a straight line. Such a small section of the Sumner circle is known as a "position line."

The desired track is laid out on the chart, and the "Dead Reckoning" position for the time of the solar observation is indicated on it. The track should be intersected at this point by the position line, the observation thus forming a check upon the "Dead Reckoning."

The altitude of the sun or of a star is measured by the sextant. For such an observation to be exact, it is necessary that not only should the sun or stars be viewed clearly, but that a clear horizon, formed either by the ocean or by suitable clouds, should be visible.

Corrections must be applied to the observed altitude for the aircraft's height above the horizon, for refraction, and for the diameter of the body under observation—the latter two corrections being given in the nautical almanac. There may be, also, an error inherent in the sextant itself. For extremely refined navigation, corrections are applied in accordance with the direction and velocity of the aeroplane or airship; but these are not really necessary, since navigation of aircraft does not require such close calculation.

When the sun or star observed is directly south of the aerial navigator in the northern hemisphere, or north of him in the southern hemisphere, the altitude, corrected for declination of the body under observation, gives the aircraft's latitude. When the navigator is directly east or west, the altitude, corrected for the time of observation, gives its longitude.

If the horizon is invisible, owing to fogs or unsuitable clouds, it may be replaced by means of a spirit level; but great care should be taken in making such observations, since a spirit level on an aeroplane or airship is not wholly reliable, unless the craft is proceeding in an absolutely straight direction, and without sway of any kind.

All methods of navigation by Astronomical Observation fail when the sky is obscured by clouds and the heavenly bodies cannot be seen. As a general rule this drawback does not hamper air navigation to any great extent, since aircraft should be able to climb above most of the obscuring clouds. Yet it may happen, as it did in the case of our transatlantic flight, that the clouds are

HOT COFFEE WAS TAKEN ABOARD

SLOW RISING NEARLY CAUSED DISASTER AT THE START OF THE
GREAT FLIGHT

too high for such a manoeuvre.

If it were possible to measure accurately the true bearing of the sun or star at the moment of observation, then a single observation of a single heavenly body would fix the position of the craft at the intersection of the line of bearing with the position line. At the time of writing, however, there are no satisfactory means of making such a measurement with the required degree of accuracy. Apparatus which will enable this to be done is now in course of development. Navigation by means of astronomical observation will thereby be simplified greatly.

NAVIGATION BY WIRELESS DIRECTION FINDER

With the great improvements that have been made in the year 1919, the guiding of aircraft by directional wireless telegraphy is rapidly becoming a reliable and accurate means of aerial navigation. Although complicated in design and construction, the complete receiving equipment for aircraft is now light, compact, and simple of operation.

The receiving equipment on aeroplanes and airships is arranged so as to indicate, with a comparatively high degree of accuracy, the direction from which wireless signals are received. The position of the sending, or beacon, station being known, the bearing of the aircraft from that station may be plotted on a suitable chart, in which small segments of great circles are represented by straight lines. Simultaneous bearings on two known beacon stations are sufficient to fix the observer's position with tolerable accuracy at the intersection of the lines of bearing, provided that they intersect at a reasonable angle—45 degrees or more, where possible.

With the very close tuning rendered possible by the use of continuous waves, beacon stations of the future will probably be provided with automatic means whereby directional signals can be sent out at intervals of one hour or less. Such signals will be coded, so that the crews of aircraft can identify the wireless station. The wave lengths must be chosen so as not to interfere with messages sent from commercial stations.

If there be a beacon station at the air navigator's destination, it is possible for him to direct his course so that the craft is always headed for the beacon; and in due time he will reach his objective.

This simple but lazy method, however, is not to be recommended; for, owing to the action of the wind, the route covered is longer than the straight course. To counteract drift and proceed in a direct line towards his destination, the air navigator frequently has to direct his course so that the craft is not headed straight for the objective. Hence, with a single beacon station, frequent observations of drift are necessary, if the shortest route is to be followed. Thus:

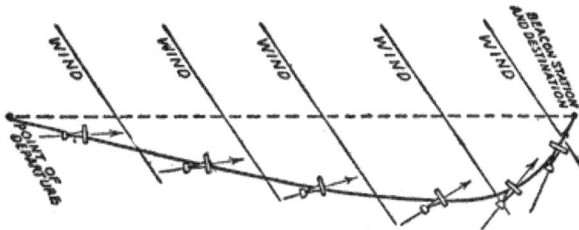

Approximate path taken by aircraft headed always towards beacon station.

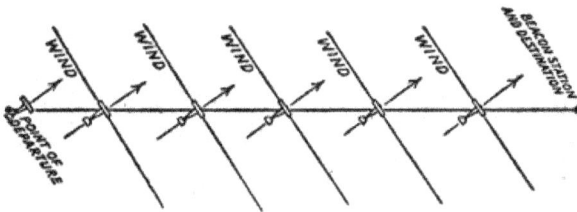

Path taken by aircraft headed so as to counteract drift.

When two or more beacon stations are available, and positions can be ascertained at least once an hour, observation on the surface of the ocean for drift, although desirable, is not absolutely necessary. The drift may be calculated with accuracy enough from the craft's position as found by the lines of bearing indicated in messages from the various beacon stations.

Another method of employing the Wireless Direction Finder is for aircraft to send out signals to two or more beacon stations, which reply by advising the air navigator of his bearing in relation to themselves. This is, perhaps, the most accurate method. Its disadvantage lies in the fact that whereas the heavier and more robust apparatus needed for it can easily be employed in the stationary beacon stations, few aircraft will be able to support wireless sending apparatus of sufficient weight to carry over the long distances they must cover in trans-oceanic aerial travel.

The greatest advantage of air navigation by means of wireless telegraphy is that it can be employed in any weather. Fogs and clouds do not make it inoperative, nor even less accurate. Another recommendation is that its use does not entail a knowledge of advanced mathematics, as required for navigation by astronomical observation.

I believe firmly that the air navigator of the future will rely upon the Wireless Direction Finder as his mainstay, while using astronomical observation and the system of "Dead Reckoning" as checks upon the wireless bearings given him, and as second and third strings to his bow, in case the wireless receiving apparatus breaks down.

CHAPTER 10

The Future of Transatlantic Flight

Although three pioneer flights were made across the Atlantic during the summer of 1919, the year passed without bringing to light any immediate prospect of an air service between Europe and America. Nor does 1920 seem likely to produce such a development on a regular basis.

Before a transatlantic airway is possible, much remains to be done—organisation, capitalization, government support, the charting of air currents, the establishment of directional wireless stations, research after improvements in the available material. All this requires the spending of money; and for the moment neither governments nor private interests are enamoured of investments with a large element of speculation.

But, sooner or later, a London-New York service of aircraft must be established. Its advantages are too tremendous to be ignored for long. Prediction is ever dangerous; and, meantime, I am confining myself to a discussion of what can be done with the means and the knowledge already at the disposal of experts, provided their brains are allied to sufficient capital.

Notwithstanding that the first two flights across the Atlantic were made respectively by a flying-boat and an aeroplane, it is very evident that the future of transatlantic flight belongs to the airship. That the apparatus in which Sir John Alcock and I made the first non-stop air journey over the Atlantic was an aeroplane only emphasises my belief that for long flights above the ocean the dirigible is the only useful vehicle. If science discovers some startlingly new motive power—for example, intermolecular energy—that will revolutionize mechanical propulsion, heavier-than-air craft may be as valuable for long flights as for air traffic over shorter distances. Until then trans-ocean flying on a commercial basis must be monopolised by lighter-than-air craft.

The aeroplane—and in this general term I include the flying boat and the seaplane—is impracticable as a means of transport for distances over one thousand miles, because it has definite and scientific limitations of size, and consequently of lift. The ratio of weight to power would prevent a forty-ton aeroplane—which is approximately the largest heavier-than-air craft that at present might be constructed and effectively handled—from remaining aloft in still air for longer than twenty-five hours, carrying a load of passengers and mails of about five tons at an air speed of, say, eighty-five miles an hour. Its maximum air distance, without landing to replenish the fuel supply, would thus be two thousand, one hundred and twenty-five miles. For a flight of twenty-five hundred miles all the disposable lift (gross lift minus weight of structure) would be needed for crew and fuel, and neither passengers nor freight could be taken aboard.

There is not in existence an aeroplane capable of flying, without alighting on the way, the three thousand miles between London and New York, even when loaded only with the necessary crew. With the very smallest margin of safety no transatlantic route of over two thousand miles is admissible for aeroplanes. This limitation would necessitate time-losing and wearisome journeys between London and Ireland, Newfoundland and New York, to and from the nearest points on either side of the ocean. Even under these conditions only important mail or valuable articles of little weight might be carried profitably.

As against these drawbacks, the larger types of airships have a radius far wider than the Atlantic. Their only limit of size is concerned with landing grounds and sheds; for the percentage of useful lift increases with the bulk of the vessel, while the weight to power ratio decreases. A voyage by dirigible can therefore be made directly from London to New York, and far beyond it, without a halt.

Another advantage of lighter-than-air craft is that whereas

the restricted space on board an aeroplane leaves little for comfort and convenience, a large rigid airship can easily provide first-rate living, sleeping and dining quarters, besides room for the passengers to take exercise by walking along the length of the inside keel, or on the shelter deck. In a saloon at the top of the vessel no noise from the engines would be heard, as must be the case in whatever quarters could be provided on a passenger aeroplane.

Yet another point in favour of the airship as a medium for trans-ocean flight is its greater safety. An aeroplane is entirely dependent for sustentation in the air on the proper working of all its motors. Should two motors—in some cases even one—break down, the result would be a forced descent into the water, with the possibility of total loss on a rough sea, even though the craft be a solid flying boat. In the case of an airship the only result of the failure of any of the motors is reduction of speed. Moreover, a speed of four-fifths of the maximum can still be maintained with half the motors of an airship out of action, so that there is no possibility of a forced descent owing to engine breakdown. The sole result of such a mishap would be to delay the vessel's arrival. Further, it may be noted that an airship's machinery can be so arranged as to be readily accessible for repairs and replacement while on a voyage.

As regards comparative speed the heavy type of aeroplane necessary to carry an economical load for long distances would not be capable of much more than eighty-five to ninety miles an hour. The difference between this and the present airship speed of sixty miles an hour would be reduced by the fact that an aeroplane must land at intermediate stations for fuel replenishment. Any slight advantage in speed that such heavier-than-air craft possess will disappear with the future production of larger types of dirigible, capable of cruising speeds varying from seventy-five to ninety miles an hour. For the airship service London-New York direct, the approximate time under normal conditions should be fifty hours. For the aeroplane service London-Ireland-Newfoundland-New York the time would be at least forty-six hours.

Perhaps the most convincing argument in favour of airships as against aeroplanes for trans-ocean aviation is that of comparative cost. All air estimates under present conditions must be very approximate; but I put faith in the carefully prepared calculations of experts of my acquaintance. These go to show that, with the equipment likely to be available during the next few years, a regular and effective air service between London and New York will need (again emphasising the factor of approximation) the following capital and rates:

	Airship Service[1]	Aëroplane Service[2]
Capital required	$13,000,000	$19,300,000
Passenger rate:		
London-New York....	$240	$575
Rate per passenger:		
Mile	8 cents	18 cents
Mails per ounce:		
London-New York.....	6¼ cents	15½ cents

1. For airships with gross gas capacity of 3,500,000 cubic feet and total load of 105 tons.

2. For machines with total load of 40 tons.

These figures for an airship service are based on detailed calculations, of which the more important are:

Capital Charges:

Four airships of 3,500,000 cu. ft. capacity, at $2,000,000 each..........	$8,000,000
Two double airship sheds at $1,500,000 each	3,000,000
Land for two sheds and aërodromes at $150,000 each	300,000
Workshops, gas plants, and equipment.	750,000
Working capital, including spare parts, stores, etc.	850,000
Wireless equipment	50,000
Miscellaneous accessories	50,000
Total capital required..............	$13,000,000
Annual charge, interest at 10%.......	$1,300,000

80

Depreciation and Insurance:

Airships.

Useful life, about 3 years.

Obsolete value, about $100,000 per ship.

Total depreciation per ship, $1,900,000 in three years.

Average total depreciation per annum for four ships for 3 years, $2,535,000.

Airship sheds.

Total annual charge...............	$90,000

Workshops and plant.

Depreciation at 5% per annum......	17,500
Total annual charge for depreciation....	2,650,000
Total annual insurance charges on airships and plant...................	617,500

Annual Establishment Expenses:

Salaries of Officers and Crews—

4 airship commanders $20,000		
8 airship officers 30,000		
Total number crew hands (64) 80,000	$130,000	
	$130,000	

Salaries of Establishment—

Management and Staff.......$25,000		
Workshop hands, storekeepers, etc. (50 at each shed—total 100) 100,000	$125,000	

Total annual establishment expenses....	$255,000

Repairs and Maintenance:

Sheds and plant, annual charge, say....	$25,000
Repairs and overhaul of airships.......	100,000
Total charge	$125,000

Total annual charges on above basis.....$4,947,500
Say $5,000,000

Cost Chargeable per Crossing:

Taking the total number of crossings per year as 200 (London-NewYork)—

Proportion of annual charges per crossing	$25,000
Petrol per trip, 30 tons at $125 per ton.	3,750
Oil per trip, 2 tons at $200 per ton......	400
Hydrogen used, 750,000 cu. ft. at $2.50 per 1,000 cu. ft....................	1,875

Cost of food per trip for crew of 19 and
100 passengers 2,000

Total charge per crossing (London-New
York) $33,025

The weight available for passengers and mails on each airship of the type projected would be fifteen tons. This permits the carrying of one hundred and forty passengers and effects, or ten tons of mails and fifty passengers. To cover the working costs and interest, passengers would have to be charged $240 per head and mails $2,025 per ton for the voyage London-New York.

This charge for passengers is already less than that for the more expensive berths on transatlantic liners. Without a doubt, with the coming of cheaper fuel, lower insurance rates and larger airships, it will be reduced eventually to the cheapest rate for first-class passages on sea liners.

With a fleet of four airships, a service of two trips each way per week is easily possible. For aeroplanes with a total load of forty tons the weight available for passengers and mails is 2.1 tons. If such a craft were to carry the same weekly load as the service of airships—thirty tons each way—it would be necessary to have fourteen machines continually in commission. Allowing for one hundred *per cent.* spare craft as standby for repairs and overhaul, twenty-eight aeroplanes would be required. The approximate cost of such a service is:

Capital Charges:

28 aëroplanes at $600,000 each........$16,750,000
28 aëroplane sheds at $50,000 each... 1,400,000
Land for 4 aërodromes...............   500,000
Workshops and equipments...........   100,000
Spare parts, etc....................   500,000
Wireless equipment   50,000

Total capital required...........$19,300,000
Annual charge at 10% interest........ $1,930,000

Depreciation and Insurance:
Aëroplanes.
Useful life, say 3 years, as for airships.
Obsolete value, say, $30,000 per machine. Average total depreciation per annum for 28 machines.......$5,250,000

Aëroplane Sheds.

Total annual charge................ 60,000

Workshops and Plant.

Depreciation at 3% per annum....... 3,000

Total annual charge for depreciation.... 5,314,000

Total annual insurance charges on machinery and plant................1,152,000

Annual Establishment Expenses:

Salaries of 36 pilots at $3,000 per annum $108,000

Salaries of 36 engineers at $2,000 per annum 72,000

Salaries of 12 stewards at $1,500 per annum 18,000

Salaries of establishment—

Management and staff............... 25,000

Workshop hands and storekeepers, etc., 100 off 100,000

Total annual establishment expenses... $323,000

Repairs and Maintenance:

Sheds and plant, annual charge, say..... $25,000

Repairs and overhaul to machines....... 50,000

Total $75,000

Total annual charges on above basis...$8,792,500

Cost chargeable per crossing:

Proportion of annual charges per crossing.. $7,250

Petrol used per trip, 28 tons at $125 per ton 3,500

Oil per trip, 2 tons at $200 per ton........ 400

Cost of food per trip for 29 passengers and crew of seven........................ 500

$11,650

It will be seen from the above that the direct running cost is 38%, and the overhead charges 62% of the total cost.

With a weight of 2.1 tons available on each machine for passengers and mails twenty passengers might be carried. To cover the working costs and interest they must be charged $575 per head. The rate for mails would be $5,500 per ton.

Having made clear that the airship is the only means of transatlantic flight on a paying basis, the next point to be considered is the type of dirigible necessary. A discussion at present of the size of the airships that will link Europe and America can be lit-

LUCKY JIM AND TWINKLETOE, THE MASCOTS

THE TRANSATLANTIC FLIGHT ENDED WITH A CRASH IN AN IRISH BOG

tle more substantial than guesswork. The British dirigible *R-34*, which last year made the famous pioneer voyage between England and the United States, is too small for commercial purposes, with its disposable lift of twenty-nine tons and its gas capacity of less than two million cubic feet. Experts have predicted the use of airships of five million and ten million cubic feet capacity, with respective weights of thirty tons and one hundred tons available for passengers and freight.

It is probable, however, that such colossi must await birth for many years, and that a beginning will be made with moderate-sized craft of about three million, five hundred thousand cubic feet capacity, similar to those that serve as the basis of the estimates for a service between London and New York. A combination of British interests is planning to send ships of this type all over the world. These can be built immediately, and there are already in existence suitable sheds to house them. Details of their structure and capabilities may be of interest.

The projected airship of three million, five hundred thousand cubic feet capacity is capable of carrying a useful load of fifteen tons (passengers and mails) for a distance of forty-eight hundred miles in eighty hours, at the normal cruising speed. The total lifting power is one hundred and five tons, and the disposable lift (available for fuel, oil, stores, crew, passengers and freight) is sixty-eight tons. The maximum engine power is thirty-five hundred h. p., the maximum speed seventy-five miles an hour.

The normal flying speed, using a cruising power of two thousand h. p., is sixty miles an hour. The overall length is eight hundred feet, the maximum diameter and width one hundred feet, and the overall height one hundred and five feet. These particulars and performances are based on present design, and on the results attained with ships of two million cubic feet capacity, now in service. The figures are conservative, and it is probable that a disposable lift greater than that of the specifications will be obtained as a result of improved structural efficiency.

The passenger accommodation will be such that the air journey can be made in comfort equal to that on a first-class liner of the sea. Apart from their comparatively small disposable lift, a main objection to vessels of the *R-34* type for commercial purposes is that the living quarters are in cars slung from under the middle envelope. In this position they are necessarily rather cramped. In the proposed craft of three million, five hundred thousand cubic feet capacity the passengers' quarters are at the top of the vessel. There, they will be roomy and entirely free from the vibration of the engines. They are reached through an internal corridor across the length of the ship, or by elevator, from the bottom of it.

The main room is a large saloon lounge fitted with tables and chairs in the style of a Pullman car. Around it are windows, allowing for daylight and for an outlook in every direction. Part of it is fire-proofed, and serves as a smoking room.

Next to, and communicating with, the lounge is the dining saloon. This leads to a serving hatch and electrical cooking apparatus. Electrical power is provided by dynamos driven off the main engines. Current for electric lighting and heating of the saloons, cars and sleeping quarters is provided by the same method.

Sleeping accommodation is in four-berth and two-berth cabins on top of the airship and forward of the living saloons. The cabins are of the type and size fitted on ocean-going steamers. With them are the usual bathrooms and offices. Other conveniences are an open shelter deck at the vessel's aft end, to enable passengers to take the air, and an observation car, fitted below the hull and also at the aft end, so that they can observe the land or sea directly below them.

No danger from fire need be feared. The machinery installation is carefully insulated from the gas bags, and the quarters are to be rendered fire-proof and gas-proof. Moreover, the amount of weight involved by the passengers' section is so small, compared with the weight of the machinery, fuel, cargo and stores, carried in the lower part of the craft, that the stability of the ship for rolling is unaffected by the novel position of the living quarters.

The ship's officers will have on the hull, towards the forward end, a control and navigation compartment, containing the main controls, navigation instruments, charts, and a cabin for the wireless telegraphy installation. The windows of this car give a clear view in every direction.

Other general specifications are:

Hull Structure.—The shape of the hull is of the most perfect stream-line form within the limitations of constructional requirements. An internal keel corridor, running along the bottom of the hull, contains all petrol and oil tanks and the water ballast.

Outer Covering.—The outer cover is made of special weather-proof fabric, which gives the longest possible life. This fabric is as efficient as possible in insulating the gas from change of temperature, and thus avoids great variations in the lift.

Gasbags.—The gas capacity is divided up into gasbags made of suitable rubber-proofed cotton fabric, lined with gold-beaters' skins. Gasbags will be fitted to automatic relief valves and hand control manoeuvring valves.

Machinery Cars.—Six machinery cars are provided, each containing one engine installation, with a direct-driven propeller fitted at the aft end. These compartments give the mechanics easy access to each of the six engines, and allow them to handle all parts of the machinery. Engine room telegraphs of the electrical type communicate between the forward compartment and each of the machinery cars.

Whereas the living quarters and the control compartment must be heated by electric radiators, arrangements can be made to warm the machinery cars by utilising the exhaust heat. The transmission gear in two of the wing cars is to be fitted with reversing gear, so that the craft may be driven astern. So that passengers shall not be worried by the usual roar of the exhaust, special silencers will be fitted. The transmission gear is also so arranged that all unnecessary clamour from it may be avoided.

The engines run on gasoline fuel, but they have devices whereby they can be run alternatively on hydrogen gas. They are designed to develop their maximum power at a height of five thousand feet.

Telephones.—Telephone communication links all stations on

the airship.

Landing Gear.—Inflated buffer landing bags of a special type are to be fitted underneath the Forward Control Compartment and underneath the two Aft Machinery Cars. These enable the airship to alight either on land or on the sea's surface.

Wireless Telegraphy.—A powerful wireless telegraphy installation is to be fitted in the wireless cabin in the forward control compartment. It will have a range for sending and receiving of at least five thousand miles.

Crew.—Two watches would be required, taking duty in eight-hour shifts. Both must be on duty when the craft leaves or lands. Each watch consists of navigating officer, steersman, elevator man, four engineers and a wireless operator. With the commanding officer and two stewards, whose duties are not regulated by watches, the crew thus numbers nineteen men.

Although the speed of the airship at maximum power is seventy miles per hour, the crossing normally would be made at sixty miles per hour, which only requires two thousand horse power, and is much more economical in fuel. The full speed, however, can be used whenever the ship is obliged to voyage through storm areas or against strong head winds.

By the Azores route, the time needed for the journey of thirty-six hundred miles, at a speed of sixty miles per hour, is sixty hours; but to allow for delays owing to adverse weather, the airship would always carry eighty hours' fuel, allowing for a speed of sixty miles per hour. The normal time for the journey from London to New York, *via* Portugal and the Azores (thirty-six hundred miles) would be, therefore, two and one half days. The normal time for the journey New York to London by the direct route (three thousand miles) would be just over two days.

The prevailing wind on the direct route is almost always from West to East, which favours the Eastbound journey, but is unfavourable to the Westbound journey. It is proposed that the crossing Eastward from New York to London be made by the most direct route, advantage thus being taken of the Westerly winds.

By making the Westbound journey on the Southerly route, *via* the Coast of Portugal and the Azores, and on 35' N. parallel of latitude across the Atlantic, and then to New York, the voyage is made in a region where the prevailing Westerly winds of the higher latitudes are absent, and only light winds are encountered, generally of a favourable direction. This route, however, adds about six hundred miles to the distance. With a ship speed of sixty miles per hour, it would be quicker to make the West-bound journey by the direct route if the Westerly wind did not exceed ten miles per hour. If the wind were greater, time would be saved by covering the extra six hundred miles of the Southerly route and dodging the unfavourable air currents.

With four airships on the Cross-Atlantic airway, two only would be in service at a time, so that each could lay up during alternate weeks for overhaul and re-fit. As the time of journey between London and New York will vary between fifty to sixty hours, each airship can easily make two crossings or one double journey per week, thus giving a service, with two dirigibles, of two "sailings" each way per week.

The average time table might therefore be as follows:

LEAVE LONDON	ARRIVE NEW YORK
Monday morning	Wednesday afternoon or evening
Thursday morning	Saturday afternoon or evening
LEAVE NEW YORK	ARRIVE LONDON
Monday afternoon	Thursday morning
Thursday afternoon	Sunday morning.

From available weather reports, it is considered that crossings are practicable on at least three hundred days in the year. Probably a total of two hundred crossings in the year could be maintained. Until further study of weather conditions supplies a certain knowledge of the best possible altitudes and latitudes, it is likely that a regular service of two crossings each way per week will be maintained only in the months of May to September, and that the crossings from October to April will be irregular, the day of departure being dependent on the weather.

Weather difficulties are likely to be much less severe than might be imagined. Rain, hail and snow should have little influence on the navigation of airships. An outer covering that is rainproof and non-absorbent avoids the absorption of water and the consequent increase of weight. Hail and snow cannot adhere to the surface of the craft when in flight, owing to its high speed through the air; and, in any case, the precipitation height being not more than eight thousand feet, they can be avoided by flying above this altitude.

Fog may give trouble in landing, but during the journey an airship can keep above it. If the terminal were enveloped by fog an arriving ship could pass on to an emergency landing ground away from the fog-belt; if the mistiness were slight, it could remain in the air until the ground were visible, making use of its margin of fuel beyond the amount necessary for the London-New York flight. Airships in fog may be enabled to find their landing ground by means of captive balloons or kites, and of strong searchlights from the ground. At night, the balloons or kites could carry electric lights, with connections from the aerodrome.

In any case, fog, rain, hail and snow are nearly always local in their occurrence, and can be avoided by a short deviation from the usual route. Atlantic records indicate that on the main steamship routes fog sufficient to impede navigation does not occur on more than about twelve days in the year.

Wind is a factor that needs more careful study in its relation to transatlantic air navigation. In most cases, unduly strong winds can be dodged by flying on a higher level, or by cruising on a different course, so as to avoid the storm belt. Heavy storms, which are usually of a cyclonic nature, rarely cover an area of more than two hundred miles diameter. Moreover, the rate of progression of a cyclonic area is much less than the speed of the air movement. An airship is able to shake off a cyclonic area by a deviation from its course of not more than two hundred miles. Once away from the storm belt, it has no difficulty in keeping clear of it.

When higher levels of the air have been charted, there is every reason to believe that the known movements of the Atlantic winds will be used to shorten air journeys. There are at sea level, between certain clearly defined latitudes, prevailing winds of constant direction. At greater heights, also, there is in most latitudes a constant drift which, if charted, might be useful even if winds at sea level were unfavourable.

Although precise information is available of the prevailing and periodic winds at sea level in various latitudes, very little coordinated work appears to have been done in charting the prevailing and seasonal winds in higher levels of the atmosphere. Observations of the air currents over various localities in the United States, England and Germany have been taken, but very little is known of the winds above the great ocean tracts. There is a great necessity for international research to provide data for predictions of weather conditions in the upper atmosphere and thus enable advantage to be taken of these higher currents.

At high altitudes, constant winds of from thirty to forty miles per hour are common. If the prevailing directions of those were known to airship navigators, the duration of the journey could be considerably shortened, even if this meant taking an indirect route. It is undesirable to fly at great heights owing to the low temperature; but with suitable provision for heating there is no reason why flying at ten thousand feet should not be common.

Air currents cannot be charted as exactly as sea currents; but much valuable work can and will be done by tabulating in detail, for the guidance of air navigators, the tendencies of the Atlantic atmospheric drifts. Reliable charts, used in conjunction with directional messages from wireless stations and ships, may make it possible for vessels on the London-New York air service always to avoid troublesome winds, as well as storms and fogs, and to reduce the percentage of risk to a figure not exceeding that relative to sea liners.

For the rest, the excellence of the most modern engines and the fact that one or two, or even three of them can be temporarily out of action without affecting the airship's stability during a flight, minimize the danger of a breakdown from loss of power. The only remaining obstacle to reasonable safety would seem to be in landing on and departing from the terminal during rough weather. This can be overcome by the recently patented Vickers

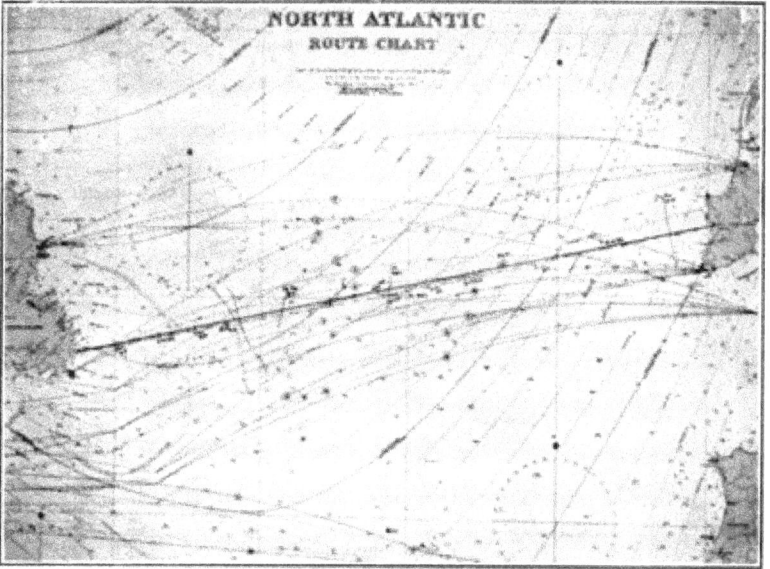

CHART OF THE NORTH ATLANTIC SHOWING COURSE OF THE FLIGHT

THE MEN WHO WORKED WITHOUT GLORY
TO MAKE THE FLIGHT POSSIBLE

Mooring Gear for Rigid Airships.

The gear, designed so as to permit an airship to land and remain moored in the open for extended periods in any weather without the use of sheds, consists principally of a tall steel mast or tower, about one hundred and fifty feet in height, with a revolving head to which the craft is rigidly attached by the nose, permitting it to ride clear of the ground and to turn round in accordance with the direction of the wind. It is provided with a hauling-in winch and rope to bring the ship up to the mooring point.

An elevator, for passengers and goods, runs up the tower from the ground to the platform adjoining the nose of the airship. The passengers reach their quarters along a passage through the vessel, and the goods are taken down a runway. An airship moored to this mast can remain unharmed in even the worst weather, and need be taken into a shed only when overhaul and repairs are necessary.

In discussing the future of transatlantic flight, I have confined myself to the projected service between London and New York. There is likely to be another route over the Atlantic—London to Rio de Janeiro, *via* Lisbon and Sierra Leone. Already in London tickets are on sale at $5,000 apiece for the first flight from London to Rio. This, of course, is a freak price, which covers the distinction of being in the first airship to travel from England to Brazil. If and when a regular London-Rio service is established, the ordinary passenger rate should be little more than the $240 estimated as the air fare on the London-New York route.

It may be that the London-New York air service will not arrive for many years. Sooner or later, however, it must arrive; for science, allied to human enterprise, never neglects a big idea. It may be that, when it does arrive, the structure of the craft and the methods of navigation applied to them will differ in important details from what I have indicated. I make no pretence at prophecy, but have merely tried to show how, with the means already at hand, moderately priced air journeys from Europe to America can be made in two to two and a half days, with comfort, safety and a high degree of reliability. Meanwhile, much depends on the funds available for the erection of stations for directional wireless messages, on research into the air currents at various levels above the Atlantic Ocean, on the courage of capitalists in promoting what seems to be a very speculative enterprise, and on new adaptations of old mechanical inventions.

Already hundreds of aeroplanes, as time-saving vehicles, are used regularly in many countries for commercial traffic over comparatively short distances—the carriage of mails, passengers, valuable freight and urgent special journeys. When, but not until, the hundreds become thousands, and the longer distances are as well served by airships as are the shorter distances by aeroplanes, the world's air age will be in sight.

CHAPTER 11

The Air Age

Although facts disappointed many over-sanguine expectations that the billions of dollars invested in aeronautics during the war would pay direct dividends already in 1919, the year brought us a long step nearer the age of universal flight. Meantime, commercial aviation is still a long way from the stage at which bankers regard its undertakings as good security for loans.

Air routes have been opened up in most parts of the world. Captain Ross-Smith has shown, by his magnificent journey from England to Australia in a Vickers-Vimy aeroplane, that long-distance flights over the most out-of-the-way lands and ocean tracts can be made even under the present unsatisfactory conditions, before terminals, landing grounds and wireless stations are provided for air pilots and navigators.

The Atlantic has been crossed four times, twice by a dirigible, once by an aeroplane and once by a flying boat. Aeroplanes have flown from England to India. Aircraft have been used for commercial purposes in every part of Western Europe, in most countries of North and South America, in Australia, India, Egypt and South Africa. Important exhibitions of modern aircraft, similar to automobile shows, have been held in London, New York, Paris, Amsterdam and elsewhere.

Today all the Great Powers can show commercial air services in full operation. Of these the most important are perhaps the triangular airways around London, Paris and Brussels. One French and two British companies operate daily between London and Paris; British craft travel backwards and forwards between London and Brussels three times a week; and French machines fly between Paris and Brussels every day.

The London-Paris services have established a magnificent record for efficiency and regularity. Valuable and urgent freight of every kind, including furs, dresses, jewellery, documents, a bunch of keys, perfume, a grand piano and even a consignment of lobsters, have been delivered in safety. Forty pounds of assorted London newspapers are taken each morning to Paris, where they are sold in the streets on the day of publication instead of next morning, as was the case when they were forwarded by train and packet-boat. Leading London papers, such as the *Times*, the *Telegraph*, the *Morning Post*, the *Daily Mail*, and the *Daily Express*, have regular contracts with one of the companies.

As for passengers, men of every occupation take advantage of the opportunity to travel comfortably from London to Paris in two and one-quarter hours. There is seldom a vacant seat on the larger machines; although the fare is at present rather high, ranging from $75 to $105 for the single journey.

Moreover, the accommodation on two of the types of aeroplane now used—the Handley-Page *W-8* and the Airco *DH-18*—is more attractive than that of a Pullman car. The Handley-Page *W-8* carries fifteen to twenty passengers with personal luggage, or two tons of freight. The Airco *DH-18* takes eight passengers, with their personal luggage.

The past year saw no specially important developments of commercial aviation inside Great Britain itself. A week-end service between Southampton and Havre was inaugurated, and passengers and mails were flown from London to Leeds. The most important undertaking was perhaps the delivery by air of newspapers. For a time, the Manchester edition of the *Daily Mail* was taken by air for distribution in Carlisle, Dundee and Aberdeen, the last-named place being reached in three and one-quarter hours instead of the thirteen hours of train journey. Evening newspapers were carried daily during the summer from London to various resorts on the South coast.

The London-Leeds undertaking is the only regular service between English towns that has lasted for long. Elsewhere the air rates proved to be too high, and although there were plenty of aerodromes, the promoters of aerial transport companies could not compete with the all-embracing network of railways. During the great railway strike of October, however, valuable transport work was done by aircraft. For the rest, aeroplanes in England are chartered as aerial taxicabs for special trips, and last summer one or two companies reaped a moderate harvest by organising pleasure trips at the seaside resorts. An airship or two have taken tours around the battlefields of France and Flanders. A few wealthy amateurs have bought aeroplanes for their private use.

Other European countries—France, Italy, Holland, Belgium, Scandinavia, Spain and Portugal—have made rather less progress in the manufacture and development of aeroplanes or dirigibles; but their use of aircraft for commercial purposes was about the same as that of Britain—newspaper distribution, some special journeys, and many joyrides. French aviators have opened tentative airways to Morocco, Senegal and Tunis. For regular passenger or goods services in continental Europe the high cost of fuel and accessories makes the rates too high. Also, aerodromes and landing grounds are too few; and seldom can aeroplanes compete on a large scale with railways over comparatively short distances. Exceptions are the Paris-Lyons and Madrid-Lisbon airways.

Germany, throughout what was for her a terrible year, made further progress with her Zeppelin dirigibles. A number of return voyages were made over the route Berlin-Munich-Vienna-Constantinople. The latest type of Zeppelin is so efficient that no weather conditions, except a strong cross-hangar wind, prevents the airship *Bodensee* from making its daily flight of three hundred and ninety miles between Friedrichshafen and Staalsen, thirteen miles from Berlin. The passenger carrying Zeppelins, which prior to the war provided the only important example of commercial aircraft, claim a remarkable record. They have carried more than one hundred and forty thousand people, and yet not one of the passengers has been killed or injured in an accident; although some members of the crews lost their lives in the early days of the pioneer Zeppelins.

The vast distances of the United States offer better opportunities for aeroplane traffic than the comparatively small and closely-railwayed countries of Western Europe. There is no doubt that, had the United States government supported its aircraft companies to the same extent as did the British Government, commercial aviation in America would have travelled along a smooth road.

Even without this support it has made excellent progress. Successful regular services are established between Los Angeles and San Diego, and elsewhere in the West, and in the East many passengers have been carried between New York and Atlantic City, and around the coast of Florida. Plans are being laid for various other airways, including one between Key West and Havana.

While no continuous service for aerial goods traffic exist in the United States, aeroplanes are often chartered for special deliveries. This is particularly the case in the oil countries of Texas and Oklahoma, where newly-grown and important centres are off the beaten railroad track. One company in Oklahoma regularly sends its employees' pay by aeroplane from town to oilfield camp, thus assuring a quick and safe delivery, free from the necessity of armed guards and the danger of hold-ups.

Other items worth noting in the United States' aerial history of the past twelve months are that aeroplanes have performed survey work and located forest fires, that thirty-two cities have applied for commercial aerodromes for postal, passenger and express purposes, and that an advertising agency is soliciting aerial business that will include display work on dirigibles, balloons and aeroplanes, the dropping of pamphlets from the air, and aerial photography.

Where the United States undoubtedly leads the way is in the ownership and use of privately owned aeroplanes—a circumstance partly explained by the great quantities of new money being spent. For a time some of the American manufacturers were months behind their post-war orders, and were selling everything that could fly. One famous company disposed of hundreds of pleasure craft at $7,500 apiece. Many buyers, impatient of delay, accepted immediate delivery of training machines, rather than wait for the pleasure craft. Reputable agencies dealing in second-hand aeroplanes bought from the United States and Canadian governments, disposed of thousands of machines and could not obtain enough to satisfy all their clients. An interesting development was the idea of community aeroplanes, purchased and maintained jointly by small groups of people living in the same residential district.

The United States postal authorities have satisfactorily maintained aerial mail services over the route New York-Washington-Cleveland-Chicago. After some preliminary fiascos these became reliable, besides being very speedy, as compared with train schedules. For June the Washington-New York air mail achieved ninety-nine *per cent.* efficiency, and the Cleveland-Chicago route one hundred *per cent.* The latter never missed a day in May and June, and not a single forced landing occurred during the first seventy days. At the close of 1919 the air mails showed a surplus of $19,000 of revenue over working costs, on a basis of two cents charge for each ounce of mail matter carried. Better results are expected now that specially constructed machines, with freight capacities of one thousand pounds and upward, are ready for use.

The British dominions and dependencies take a great interest in aeronautics, and last year saw satisfactory beginnings in some of them. In Australia, for example, a passenger and freight service links Sydney and Port Darwin, over a distance of twenty-five hundred miles, with intervening stations. Plans are ready for regular flights from North to South of the continent, and also from East to West, across the difficult country between New South Wales and Victoria on the one hand, and Western Australia on the other.

Canada has found a highly successful use for aeroplanes in prospecting the Labrador timber country. A group of machines returned from an exploration with valuable photographs and maps of hundreds of thousands of dollars' worth of forest land. Aerial fire patrols, also, have been sent out over the forests. While no important air route for passenger carrying is yet utilised in Canada, there is a certain amount of private flying, and air journeys for business purposes are common. Plans have been prepared for a regular service between Newfoundland and cities on the mainland, thus saving many hours over the time schedules perpetrated by the little Newfoundland railway.

In the South African Union, where the railway system by no means corresponds with the vast distances, many passengers and mails are carried by air from Johannesburg to Pretoria, Maritzburg, Durban and Cape Town. Later, when the services over these routes are better organised, they will doubtless be extended to important centres in Rhodesia, the East Africas and what was German South-West Africa.

Aeroplanes in India take passengers over the route Calcutta-Simla in twelve to fourteen hours of cool roominess, as compared with forty-two hours of stuffy oppressiveness on a train. Other Indian air routes in preparation are Calcutta-Bombay, Calcutta-Darjeeling and Calcutta-Puri. The air fare in India averages about 11 cents a mile.

Aerodromes and landing grounds are already prepared between Egypt and India, and several machines have made the journey from Cairo to Delhi, *via* Damascus, the Syrian Desert, Bagdad, Bandar Abbas and Karachi. Elsewhere in the East—the Malay Peninsula, Singapore, Borneo, Java and China—similar routes are planned. The whole of Eastern Africa, from Cairo to Cape Town, has been mapped out for the use of aircraft, with landing grounds at short intervals.

So much for accomplishment during the past year. What the future and the near-future have in store for aeronautics is problematical, and any detailed analysis must be conjecture. The general trend of development during the next two years may be forecast, however, with a fair degree of accuracy.

Anybody who blends sane imagination with some knowledge of the history of aeronautics must realise that what has been achieved is very little in comparison with what can be achieved. It is unnecessary to make trite comparisons with the first stages of steam locomotives or motorcars.

Yet, it is folly to expect an air age now. Its coming will be delayed by the necessity of slow, painstaking research, and by the fact that in the countries which are encouraging aviation to the greatest degree, capital is no longer fluid and plentiful, and money in substantial sums cannot be risked on magnificent experiments. The cost of building fleets of dirigibles and hosts of air terminals, for example, must be enormous; and until it has been demonstrated beyond question that they will be paying propositions, financiers and investors are unlikely to be interested in their concrete possibilities on a large scale.

Unless some startling innovation—a much cheaper fuel for example, or a successful helicopter—revolutionizes commercial aviation, its near-future is unlikely to stray beyond the extension of airways over distances of about five hundred to two thousand miles. These are likely to be covered mostly by heavier-than-air craft, although, as in Germany, dirigibles will have their place.

Extension of air traffic is especially probable in industrial and agricultural countries of large area, such as the United States, Canada, Australia, India and the South American republics. Another projected development with immediate possibilities is the linking of regions that are separated by a comparatively narrow expanse of water. Obvious examples, in addition to Britain and France, are England and Ireland, the Mediterranean coast of France and the Mediterranean coast of Africa, and Florida and Cuba.

Traffic across the ocean or a great lake offers to air travel the best time-saving inducement. To connect two places separated by one hundred and fifty miles of water, an average steamship needs ten hours. A passenger on it must spend at least one night away from home, while transacting his business. An air passenger covers the same distance in one and one-half to two hours, and can return on the same day. For such transport the seaplane and the flying boat will have their chance.

Besides the carriage of passengers, mails and valuable freight, aviation will have many additional functions. Maps may be made and checked with absolute accuracy by means of aerial photography. Another important function of the aeroplane and the aerial camera is to explore and prospect undeveloped districts. In places remote from the ordinary facilities of civilization aircraft may be used for the discovery of fire, flood and lawlessness. Already the Canadian Northwest Mounted Police have captured wrongdoers by means of aeroplane patrols.

Aircraft offer particular advantages as carriers in regions where the natural obstacles on the ground prohibit railway or road transport. In Alaska valuable metals and furs are brought to civilization on sleds drawn by dogs, over paths that are circuitous and dangerous. They could be taken in safety, and with an immense saving of time, by aeroplanes fitted with skids suitable for landing on ice and snow. Again, copper is transported from mines in the Andes by llamas, which are slow and must jog over devious tracks. Aeroplanes could make the journey directly and speedily, from mine to coast, without regard to precipice, marsh or forest.

South America is likely to be a happy hunting-ground for aeronautical pioneers. The mountain-range of the Andes, which for hundreds of miles sharply divides America into two parts, gives aviation an incontestable opportunity. The eastern section of South America could be brought days nearer the western section by high-climbing aircraft, which would provide a pleasant alternative to the roundabout, uncomfortable journeying now necessary. The air mails between the two great commercial centres of South America—Rio de Janeiro and Buenos Ayres—should also save many days of valuable time. Many owners of ranches and plantations in the Argentine, Uruguay, Paraguay and Brazil are buying aeroplanes to bring their isolated, upcountry properties in closer contact with the towns.

Asia and Africa have similar geographical problems, to which air traffic might find a ready solution. Each of these continents has enormous areas that, because of the absence of good railways, are either unproductive or much less productive than their resources warrant. A few of many such cases are Turkestan, Central Arabia, parts of China, Siberia, Thibet, and the whole of Central Africa. Most of these are rich in minerals. Meanwhile, aeroplanes have flown between the desert marts of Damascus and Bagdad in eight to ten hours. These cities are not yet linked by railroad and a camel caravan over the Syrian desert covers the same route in two weeks to a month. The same conditions apply

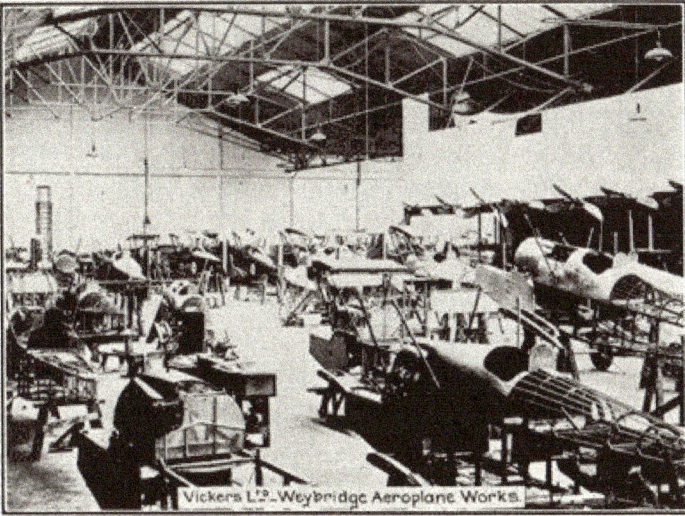

THE VICKERS AEROPLANE WORKS AT WEYBRIDGE, ENGLAND

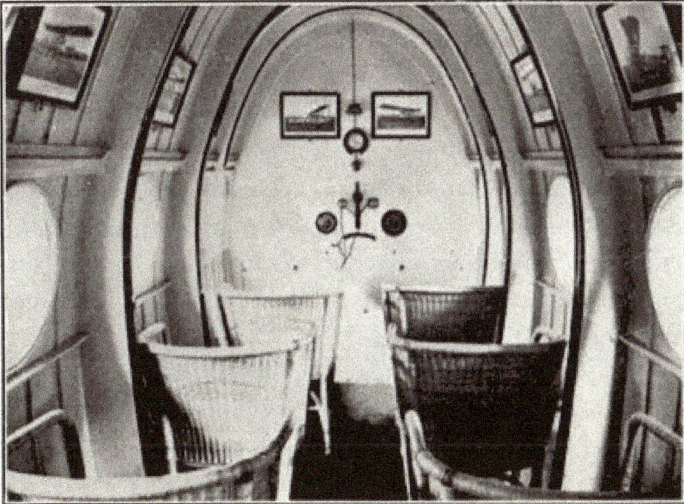

COMFORT CAN BE ENJOYED IN AIR TRAVEL TODAY

to the Gobi Desert.

So far, I have dealt with the future of commercial aeronautics almost entirely in terms of heavier-than-air machines. These— land planes, seaplanes and flying boats—have at present a useful radius of non-stop flight confined to distances of under one thousand miles. The limitation must remain until changes in the basic principles of aeroplane construction are so altered as to give a much greater speed in proportion to fuel consumption. One such change may be the introduction of wings with vari- able camber. This, by permitting variations in the angle of inci- dence, would make possible a quick ascent at a steep inclination, and a very fast forward speed once the required height had been attained. The benefits from variable camber could be increased by the introduction of a propeller with a variable pitch.

Going still further in the same direction, we may find any day that one of the attempts in various countries to design and con- struct a successful helicopter has matured, producing a machine which, by reason of a very powerful propeller on a moveable shaft that can be inclined in any direction, will not only rise and descend vertically, but also may be made to travel forward at a great speed and to perform such acrobatic tricks as sudden halts, retreats and jumps.

All this, however, is surmise; and we are faced with the fact that until the design of aeroplanes differs radically from its pre- sent form, heavier-than-air flying apparatuses are limited as to maximum size by certain structural principles too complicated for explanation in this non-technical analysis. A further limita- tion is imposed by the space needed by the largest machines for leaving the ground or landing.

Within these bounds it has been found that the maximum capacity for passengers and freight does not greatly exceed one and one-half to two tons for a non-stop journey of five hundred miles in still air. Lesser distances do not increase the useful load appreciably, but greater distances decrease it; until for a radius of about twenty-five hundred miles the whole of the disposable lift is needed for fuel, and nothing else may be carried.

For long journeys over land, therefore, the aeroplane must

come to earth for replenishment of fuel every five hundred miles. Even for this distance it cannot take more than one and one-half to two tons beyond the weight of fuel and crew. If heavier loads are to be transported, more machines must be used. Finally, there comes a point at which a single airship, carrying a heavy freight over five hundred miles, is more economical than several aeroplanes. For non-stop flights of over one thousand miles the same considerations make the airship always more economical than the aeroplane.

Over the ocean the flying boat can beat the dirigible in time and cost up to five hundred miles. Even at one thousand miles it is a commercial proposition, but it must then have all in its favour. For longer distances the airship has no competitor. It may be deduced that in years to come, when the world's airways are in general operation, heavier-than-air machines will bring freight to the great airports, there to be transferred to dirigibles and by them carried to the earth's uttermost ends.

The time for this seeming Utopia is not yet, however, although a group of airship interests in England are now planning airship services that may eventually set London within two and a half days of New York, one and a half days of Cairo, four of Rio de Janeiro, five and a half of Cape Town and seven of Australia. But first must come bold expenditure, very careful organisation, many-sided research and improved invention.

Although no claim is made that present-day airships can compete for reliability with railroad trains and ocean liners, there is no doubt that a sufficient number of passengers are prepared to pay relatively higher rates for the great saving in time taken for long distance journeys, particularly over the ocean.

The demand would be mainly for the carriage of express freight and mail matter and for passenger traffic to serve people who wish to get from centre to centre in the shortest possible time. Another use for large airships would be the carrying of freight of high intrinsic value, such as valuable ores, from places otherwise inaccessible, or not provided with other means of direct transport.

To meet the requirements of various purposes for which airships may be utilized, dirigibles of four kinds are projected:

First, the airship of moderate size and high speed for carrying express, mails and passengers.

Secondly, the air liner solely for passenger traffic, of a large size and speed.

Thirdly, the large airship of comparatively slow speed, and great carrying capacity, for general transport.

Fourthly, the small non-rigid airship for private purchase and upkeep as an aerial yacht.

The rigid airship is as yet only at the beginning of its development, particularly as regards size and carrying capacity. The airship of three million, five hundred thousand cubic feet capacity, for immediate use on the fast passenger services, carrying a load of passengers of fifteen tons for a distance of forty-eight hundred miles, might be built immediately, and could be housed in sheds at present available. As the lift and speed efficiency of a rigid airship increases rapidly in proportion to the vessel's size, it will be advantageous to use the largest airships that can be economically operated. A rigid dirigible able to carry fifty tons of passengers and freight for ten thousand miles at a speed of eighty miles an hour is quite feasible; and the design and construction of such an airship could be undertaken immediately if it were justified by the demand for air transport.

The ships of three million, five hundred thousand cubic feet capacity, which can be housed and flown for commercial purposes as soon as the required terminals and navigational facilities are ready, will approximate to those described as being suitable for a transatlantic service. If standardised for adaptation to all conditions and world routes, they should be capable of a non-stop flight of about eighty hours, at an average speed of sixty miles an hour.

To prevent wastage and reduce the running costs, several economical devices for dealing with height equilibrium are needed. On long flights the greatest problems are maintenance of the airship at a constant height, and avoidance of the loss of gas consequent on expansion when the ship rises as it loses weight by the consumption of fuel. Owing to the great variation in temperature between day and night, the ship becomes heavy at night owing to the lower temperature, and light during the day, as a result of the higher temperature. A discharge of ballast at nightfall, and of gas in the morning, is needed to keep it in equilibrium. To obviate discharge of gas, and the necessity of starting with a large weight of ballast, it is proposed to run a proportion of the engines on hydrogen fuel, so that the hydrogen can be consumed at such a rate that the loss of lift equals the loss of weight of fuel consumed by the other engines, thus economically using hydrogen which otherwise would be lost through the discharge of the gas valves.

I make the supposition that hydrogen, and not helium, will be the sustaining gas. For commercial aviation it has many advantages, for helium is dearer and rarer, and has about twenty *per cent.* less lift. Contrary to general belief, a flight in an airship filled with hydrogen, subject to proper precautions, has no greater fire risk than living near a gas factory. Helium is a necessity only for airships used in war, as, unlike hydrogen, it is not ignited by incendiary bullets from hostile aircraft. The United States has almost a monopoly of the world's quantitative supply of helium, which fact should be a tremendous asset in wartime.

The ballast difficulty can be met by apparatus to condense the water of combustion from the exhaust gases of the engines. Experiments have shown that it is practicable to recover water of slightly greater weight than the gasoline fuel consumed, thus avoiding any variation in lift due to gasoline consumption. Further, water ballast could be picked up periodically from the sea by descending and taking in water through a pump suspended from a flexible hose, or direct into tanks in the gondolas through sea-valves.

Still further reduction of running costs may be effected by fuel economy. This would be difficult with internal combustion engines of the type in use at present, for greater thermal efficiency (the ratio between the amount of heat contained in the fuel consumed and the amount of useful work delivered by the engine) necessitates heavier machinery. The reduction in gasoline consumption is thus offset by a decrease in the disposable lift. It is probable that a saving on large dirigibles might result from substituting for the internal combustion method of generating power engines that burn cheap oils. Although such engines are much heavier, and although the crude oils weigh a good deal more than gasoline, the difference would be more than covered on long flights, for gasoline is nearly four times dearer than crude oil. Moreover, the weight of oil actually consumed would be about twenty *per cent.* less than that of the gasoline burned by internal combustion engines over the same distance.

The solution may be in the employment of steam. For the rather low standards of horsepower on which dirigibles are driven, heavy steam engines of the ordinary type, although much more reliable, would be less economical than internal combustion engines, owing to the latter's better thermal efficiency. Engineers are attempting to evolve a light type of steam turbine that will overcome this drawback.

Of equal importance to fuel economy is a better system of airship navigation. This is similar in principle to steamship navigation, but it is made more complicated by the much greater drift of atmospheric currents. Moreover, air currents can never be charted as exactly as sea currents. An excellent meteorological organisation, for reporting motions of the air at given times, is therefore essential.

When flying over land a navigator can determine the drift of his vessel by taking observation on a suitable fixed point on the earth's surface, and adjusting his compass course accordingly. It is probable that a gyroscopic compass will be the standard type for dirigibles. Many aviators have experienced difficulties with the magnetic compass on long flights; although it has served me well always, especially on my transatlantic flight as Captain Alcock's navigator.

Over the sea no fixed point is available, so that the motion of the wind must be checked periodically. One method is for the navigator to make astronomical observations, and from them deduce his position on the chart. Another may be the use of bombs which ignite on the water and give out a dense smoke or a bright light, lasting for several minutes. During the day the navigator sights on the smoke, and during the night on the light, and thus discovers the wind's velocity and direction. An invention that could simplify navigation would be some form of ground-speed meter, showing at a glance the rate of progress over the earth (as distinct from air speed), with either a following or a contrary wind.

The most valuable means of airship navigation will be that of directional wireless. Communication from two separate stations, which could be either land terminals or stationary ships in the ocean, gives the direction of the transmitted wireless waves and signals to the dirigible its bearings. The position is then laid off on the chart, and the course regulated accordingly. This method was used by the German Zeppelins during the war.

Of equal importance to the structural and navigational equipment of airships is the provision of suitable terminals for each route. These would require, among other necessities, an aerodrome of about one mile square; a double airship shed capable of housing two vessels; a mooring-out tower; mechanical gear for transferring an airship from the mooring tower to the shed; hydrogen generating and storage plant; repair workshops and stores; meteorological offices; wireless telegraphy installation; electrical night signalling and landing arrangements; a station on the local railway from the main part of the city; a hotel; a garage; and customs and booking offices.

The aerodrome must be a short distance from the city served by the airship service. If possible, it should be near a chemical works where hydrogen could be produced as a by-product. The ground would be preferably on a site remote from hills and other topographical features likely to cause air disturbances.

The double sheds for housing vessels of the size specified, three million, five hundred thousand cubic feet capacity, would have two berths, the minimum dimensions of each of which must be eight hundred and fifty feet long, one hundred and fifty feet wide, and one hundred and fifteen feet high. Their contents should include hydrogen filling mains and gear for slinging the airships from the roof when deflated for overhaul. Special arrangements would be made for rapid replenishment of the ships with gas, fuel, and water ballast.

If no industrial supply of hydrogen were provided by a near-by factory, the aerodrome should have a generating plant capable of producing fifty thousand cubic feet of hydrogen per hour. Gasometer storage, with a capacity of about five hundred thousand cubic feet, is also a necessity.

The meteorological office would issue weather reports for the guidance of airship navigators, and issue navigating instructions to them by means of the wireless installation. The latter should have a range of at least five thousand miles.

Each aerodrome would be provided with suitable electric light signals to indicate the position of the landing ground to incoming ships at night, as well as landing lights to point the way to the mooring tower. Trolleys running on guide rails, with electrically driven gear, could move a dirigible from the tower to the shed with a minimum of man power.

A suitable mooring tower constitutes an enormous saving of time and labour. The Vickers Patent Mooring Gear, which has been tested satisfactorily, can be worked by half a dozen men; whereas the old method of rope pulling and dragging needs two to four hundred men for landing an airship of three million, five hundred thousand cubic feet capacity.

With existing methods, a rigid airship must be housed in a suitable shed when not in flight. The danger and difficulty of removing the ship from its shed, and returning it safely thereto after a journey, restricts the number of actual flying days in the year to those on which such operations can be performed without risk of damage, although a modern rigid airship may be in the air with efficiency and perfect safety in practically any state of the weather. The Patent Mooring Gear renders the landing independent of the weather, while calling for the attendance of only six men to actuate the various mechanical devices employed.

In principle, the gear consists of a tall steel mast, of such a height that when the ship is attached by the nose it rides on an even keel at a height of upwards of one hundred feet. The mast has at the top a platform or deck. The head of the tower is entirely enclosed and contains the necessary apparatus for bringing a vessel to rest. This top portion is designed to rotate, so that a ship, when moored, may always lie directly head to wind.

Access to the upper deck of the masthead is obtained by means of an elevator, which allows passengers to enter the ship in comfort. Behind the deck is a compartment containing the landing gear. This consists of an electrically driven winding engine, fitted with about one thousand feet of the highest quality flexible steel wire rope, together with any automatic coupling. In the compartment are also pipes for the supply to the ship of hydrogen, gasoline, oil and water from the main reservoirs, situated on the ground at the foot of the mast. The vessel itself is fitted with apparatus complementary to that housed in the masthead. From the nose projects the attachment which is gripped by the automatic coupling, while in the bow is situated a storage drum and winch for six hundred feet of wire rope.

On approaching the aerodrome, the ship wirelesses its intention to land. The masthead mooring rope is then threaded through the automatic coupling, and paid out until the free end reaches the ground below. This end of the rope is attached by a shackle to the rear of a light car, which is driven away from the mast in the direction from which the ship is approaching, while the rope uncoils from the drum above. When at a distance of seven hundred or eight hundred feet from the foot of the mast the men in charge of the gear unshackle the rope, and spread landing signs that indicate to the airship pilot their position on the ground.

On arrival over the landing party, the ship's bow mooring rope is released, and runs out from the bow attachment under the influence of a weight of several hundred pounds in the form of sandbags. Two men of the party on the ground below take charge of the rope, unshackle the sandbags, and effect a junction with the mooring mast rope, which is in the hands of the remaining men of the landing party. The rope ends are coupled together by means of a self-locking coupling, which enables the junction to be made within five seconds.

The dirigible is now connected with the head of the mooring mast by a long length of steel wire rope. On receiving a signal from the ground party, the men in charge of the winding gear in the masthead haul in. As the rope tautens, ballast is discharged from the ship, which is slowly hauled into connection with the automatic coupling already set in the open position to receive the attachment on the nose. When once this coupling is closed, the mooring ropes can be dispensed with, the ship's rope being re-wound on to the storage drum in the bows.

After landing at the masthead, connection is made with the hydrogen, gasoline, oil, and water mains, and fresh gas, fuel and water ballast are placed on board, so that the ship may be kept in trim during the discharge of cargo, and so the embarkation of passengers and stores be effected.

When all is ready to leave the masthead for flight, the pulling of a lever in the automatic coupling releases the ship. The latter then draws astern and upward, under the influence of the prevailing wind, until it is well clear of the landing station and can proceed on its course.

The design of this apparatus is such that the landing of an airship is as easy in a wind as in complete calm. With its help an airship can land in any speed of wind in which it is safe to fly. Should the wind be so high (over 60 or 70 miles per hour) that the vessel cannot reach a given mast, it will always be possible to learn by wireless the nearest station at which favourable conditions allow it to come down.

The release of the ship from the mast can take place in any wind-speed. Owing to the comparatively local nature of a big storm (storms are known not to cover districts greater than two hundred miles in diameter) the vessel, after slipping its moorings, is able to circumnavigate the disturbed area by making a small initial deviation from the true course.

A part of the aerodrome should be given over to aeroplanes, used for the bringing of mails and urgent freight from places distant from the terminal. Heavier-than-air machines, in fact, will be the veins leading to the great arteries of the world's air routes, operated by dirigibles. A strong searchlight, for the guidance of aeroplane pilots flying in fog, might be necessary. Given improved landing facilities, means might be found for them to coast down the searchlight, if the ground away from it were invisible. Another method of delivering mails, before leaving for a landing ground away from the fog belt, is to drop them, attached to a parachute. When the package reaches earth, it can be located by an electric bell, which rings on impact and continues ringing.

The mail services of today, by railway and boat, can in many cases be greatly speeded up if part of a long journey be covered by aeroplane. A good instance is the route between Great Britain and South America. If a merchant in London posts three letters to correspondents in New York, Rio de Janeiro and Buenos Ayres respectively, he may have a reply from New York before the Brazil man has had time to read his communication, and four or five days before the man in the Argentine has received his. An aerial short cut to Dakar—already several machines have flown there from Paris—would lessen by six or seven days the transit time for mailbags sent from England to Rio de Janeiro or Buenos Ayres.

As long as the internal combustion engine is used in aeronautics, and mechanical failure is always a possibility to be reckoned with, the cost of maintaining aeroplane routes, even if they be only auxiliary to dirigible or steamship services, will be greatly swollen by the need of maintaining frequent landing grounds. Every ten miles would be an ideal interval for them; every twenty miles is a minimum for first-rate insurance against risk. From a height of five thousand feet, the probable average minimum elevation for commercial air navigation, a pilot can without difficulty cover a distance of five miles while planing down without the aid of motors. From ten thousand feet he can cover ten miles under the same conditions; so that at this height he would never be outside gliding distance of landing grounds prepared every twenty miles.

Given these safeguards, the element of risk in present day aviation is no greater than it was in the early days of railways and steamboats; and little, if any, greater than in modern motoring. Many people, possessing only a newspaper acquaintance with aerial affairs, still believe mechanical flight to be perilous. In exactly the same manner men shunned the infant steamboat, railway train, bicycle and motorcar. Yet, proportionately, the aeroplane and the dirigible are responsible for no more deaths than the train or the automobile. The seeming discrepancy is because so much attention is paid to air fatalities. Every weekend motorcar accidents cause scores of fatalities. Yet the death in harness of a single aviator produces more comment than all of these. Partly, no doubt, the intense horror with which humanity regards death by falling from a great height is due to its novelty among human experiences.

The airways of the world offer some pretty problems of international politics, involving commerce, rights of landing, customs duties, air smuggling, air traffic regulations and air laws. All these were dealt with in the International Aerial Commission at the Peace Conference, which agreed upon the following principles:

1. Recognition of the greatest possible freedom of aerial navigation, as far as that freedom of navigation is reconcilable with the principle of the sovereignty of each state in the air above its territory, with the security of the state affected, and in conformity with a strict enforcement of safety regulations.

2. Regulation under obligatory permits for pilots and other aeronautical personnel to be recognised mutually by the signatory states.

3. The establishment of international air rules, including signals, lights, methods of avoiding collisions and regulations for landing.

4. The recognition of the special treatment of army, navy and state machines when on duty for the state.

5. Recognition of the right to utilise all public aerodromes in other states, under a charge to be uniform for the aircraft of all nations, including the home nation.

6. Recognition of the right of crossing one country to another, with the privilege of landing, but under the reservation of the right of the state crossed to apply its local rules, and if necessary, to force the landing of the visiting machines on signal.

7. Recognition of the principle of mutual indemnity to cover damages to persons or property due to aircraft—the state of the offending machine to make reparation and then to recoup itself in any way it sees fit.

8. Recognition of the necessity of a permanent international aeronautical commission, in order to keep the development of the legal side of aviation abreast of the development of the science itself.

9. Recognition of the obligation of each state to regulate its internal legislation along the lines of the clauses of the international agreement.

The main airways of the world are still hypothetical, but some of their main terminals, in relation to the centres of industry and population and the trade routes, will certainly be London, New York, San Francisco, Tokio, Delhi, Colombo, Cairo, Cape Town, and Rio de Janeiro. In particular London, New York, Cairo and Rio de Janeiro are fitted to be great junctions for air traffic. London is the logical distribution centre for passengers and freight from North and South America bound for Continental Europe or the East. The New York terminal should link the transatlantic airways from Europe with the airways of North America.

Rio de Janeiro should perform the same function for South America, and also be the centre of seaplane traffic up the Amazon. Cairo is destined to be the junction for the air routes between Europe, Asia, Africa and Australia. From it dirigibles or aeroplanes may pass to India (via Damascus and Bagdad), to Cape Town (*via* Nairobi), to Australia (*via* Aden and Colombo, or Delhi and Singapore), and to London (*via* Algiers or some point in Southern Italy). Cairo is also likely to be an important base for seaplanes and flying boats plying up and down the tremendous waterways of the Nile and the Great Lakes.

The British Empire is especially bound up with the airways of the future. The geographical position of the Briton forces him to think in Imperial terms. In 1776 Great Britain lost her most valuable colonies largely because the Atlantic Ocean made adequate representation of the colonial interest physically impossible. Since that day cables, steamships and the wireless have helped to overcome the distances that separate the overseas dominions from the British Isles. Aircraft and well-organised British air routes should be the greatest step in the consolidation of the far-flung Empire.

To this end British official experts mapped out the stages of the aerial route to Australia from Egypt, *via* Damascus, Bagdad, Karachi, Delhi, Calcutta, Singapore and Sumatra. Although the successive landing grounds were not ready in time for Captain Ross-Smith's magnificent flight from England to Australia, the information and advice collected by the official surveyors were of inestimable value to him. It is noteworthy that nearly the whole of the proposed airway from Egypt to Australia is over British territory or the sea.

The same is true of the proposed route from Cairo to Cape Town. This was planned out very carefully by three parties of military aviators, who covered the whole length of civilized and uncivilized Africa in their search for landing grounds. The absorption of German East Africa by the South African Union makes an all British corridor for aircraft from Cairo to Cape Town, by way of Egypt, the Sudan, British East Africa, British Central Africa, German East Africa, Rhodesia, the Transvaal and Cape Colony. There is an alternative water route over the Nile, the Great Lakes, the Zambezi River and along the coast to Cape Town. Being the junction of the airways to India, Australia and South Africa, Egypt is destined to be the nerve centre of an air-linked British Empire, just as the Suez Canal has been its jugular vein.

But the laying out of great air routes to the East and South does not complete Britain's plans. She must connect them up with London—a task which is much more complicated from the standpoint of high politics, because it involves routes over the territory of other nations. An aeroplane can fly from London to Cairo via Gibraltar without passing over foreign territory or foreign territorial waters. But the air route would be long and the aerodrome bases great distances apart, in comparison with the proposed land route of two thousand miles across France, down the length of Italy and Greece and across the Mediterranean to Cairo. Such a route necessitates an entente cordiale with the nations of Western Europe, and is one of the reasons why Great Britain can never contemplate easily a loosening of the bonds that now hold together the Allies of Western Europe.

The French, for their part, are also thinking of air routes in terms of their colonial possessions. For them the international situation is much the same as for the London–Cairo airway. French pilots need not fly over foreign territory to Algiers or Morocco. A long flight across the Mediterranean, or skirting the west coast of Spain, is a possibility. But Spanish territory is the logical corridor from France to Africa. It was over Spain that a trip was made from Toulouse to Casablanca, the eighteen hundred miles being covered in eleven hours of actual flying. The ordinary postal service takes six days. For direct aerial communication with Syria, also, France must have an entente with several intervening countries.

Not only will the aeroplane connect France more closely with Africa; it will likewise bind together the various sections of France's colonial territory in Africa, The Sahara Desert will become a less formidable obstacle to intercommunication. French pilots have made experimental flights over parts of the Sahara in a search for the best routes and landing places, as links in communication between Morocco and the Ivory Coast.

When technical progress and perfected organisation place the world's main airways in operation, there will be enormous saving of time on the longer routes. The estimated time for transatlantic flights from London to New York by the three million, five hundred thousand cubic feet dirigibles is two to two and one-half days, Other likely figures for various services are as follows:

London to India and Australia:

London to Cairo	2,050 miles
Cairo to Colombo (*via* Aden)	3,400 miles
Colombo to Perth (Australia	3,150 miles

At an average speed of sixty miles per hour, and with a stop of twelve hours at each station for refuelling, the times taken would be

London to Cairo	34 hours or 1½ days
London to Colombo	34 + 12 + 58 hours = 104 hours, or 4½ days

By train and mail steamer, the journey to Ceylon at present takes fifteen days, and to Australia over thirty days.

Cairo to Cape Town:
Cairo to British East Africa (Nairobi) 2,100 miles—35 hours
Nairobi to Cape Town   2,200 miles—37 hours
Total time from Cairo to Cape Town, allowing for a break of twelve hours at Nairobi = 84 hours

Owing to variation in the weather conditions, latitude in estimating the time of arrival must be permitted in each case. Where, however, there is a saving of several days in comparison with steamship travel, the difference of a few hours matters little.

In years to come, with the development of airship transport to the most distant centres of the world, it is conceivable that no important city will be further from London than ten days' journey. The following table, as applied to a London terminal, is by no means fantastic:

To New York	2-2½ days
To San Francisco	4½ days
To Cairo	1½ days
To Colombo	4½ days
To Perth	7 days
To Nairobi	3½ days
To Cape Town	5½ days
To Rio de Janeiro	4 days

As the maximum distance of direct flight between inter-mediate stations is not more than three thousand, five hundred miles, it would be practicable to run these services with the size of airship described three million, five hundred thousand cubic feet capacity. The cost of operation for regular services would be approximately as for the Atlantic service—passengers at the rate of eight cents per mile, and mails at the rate of six cents per ounce. With the development of larger airships, carrying greater loads, the cost should be more economical.

I admit that such a near-Utopia of an air age may not be seen by the present decade, and that its attainment demands great results from science, statesmanship and business organisation. Yet even to come within sight of world intercommunication as rapid as is indicated by the signposts of present-day aeronautics would make possible an era of greater prosperity, peace and friendliness. If people, their written communications and their goods can be taken from continent to continent as quickly, or nearly as quickly, as a cablegram, the twin evils of state parochialism and international misunderstanding will less often be dragged from the cupboard in which the world's racial skeletons are kept. The airship and the aeroplane may well become a greater influence towards internationalisation than the signed covenant of the league of nations.

LEONAUR

ALSO FROM LEONAUR

AVAILABLE IN SOFTCOVER OR HARDCOVER WITH DUST JACKET

AFGHANISTAN: THE BELEAGUERED BRIGADE *by G. R. Gleig*—An Account of Sale's Brigade During the First Afghan War.

IN THE RANKS OF THE C. I. V *by Erskine Childers*—With the City Imperial Volunteer Battery (Honourable Artillery Company) in the Second Boer War.

THE BENGAL NATIVE ARMY *by F. G. Cardew*—An Invaluable Reference Resource.

THE 7TH (QUEEN'S OWN) HUSSARS: Volume 4—1688-1914 *by C. R. B. Barrett*—Uniforms, Equipment, Weapons, Traditions, the Services of Notable Officers and Men & the Appendices to All Volumes—Volume 4: 1688-1914.

THE SWORD OF THE CROWN *by Eric W. Sheppard*—A History of the British Army to 1914.

THE 7TH (QUEEN'S OWN) HUSSARS: Volume 3—**1818-1914** *by C. R. B. Barrett*—On Campaign During the Canadian Rebellion, the Indian Mutiny, the Sudan, Matabeleland, Mashonaland and the Boer War Volume 3: 1818-1914.

THE KHARTOUM CAMPAIGN *by Bennet Burleigh*—A Special Correspondent's View of the Reconquest of the Sudan by British and Egyptian Forces under Kitchener—1898.

EL PUCHERO *by Richard McSherry*—The Letters of a Surgeon of Volunteers During Scott's Campaign of the American-Mexican War 1847-1848.

RIFLEMAN SAHIB *by E. Maude*—The Recollections of an Officer of the Bombay Rifles During the Southern Mahratta Campaign, Second Sikh War, Persian Campaign and Indian Mutiny.

THE KING'S HUSSAR *by Edwin Mole*—The Recollections of a 14th (King's) Hussar During the Victorian Era.

JOHN COMPANY'S CAVALRYMAN *by William Johnson*—The Experiences of a British Soldier in the Crimea, the Persian Campaign and the Indian Mutiny.

COLENSO & DURNFORD'S ZULU WAR *by Frances E. Colenso & Edward Durnford*—The first and possibly the most important history of the Zulu War.

U. S. DRAGOON *by Samuel E. Chamberlain*—Experiences in the Mexican War 1846-48 and on the South Western Frontier.